Rediscover
Grammar

David Crystal

Cartoons by Edward McLachlan

PEARSON
Longman

Contents

Preface

The first edition of *Rediscover Grammar* appeared at a time when grammar was conspicuous by its absence from most schools, and in a communications era in which there was no World Wide Web and in which most people had had no experience of email or other electronically mediated uses of language. A lot has happened in fifteen years.

The renewed interest in grammar teaching, as part of a curriculum which now recognizes the importance of language awareness, has had several consequences, chief of which is the concern to integrate the study of language structure with that of language in use. To achieve this goal, the role of semantics and pragmatics – missing from the first edition, and introduced only briefly as part of the introduction in the 1996 revised edition – is now perceived to be central.

I have made the decision not to incorporate a semantic and pragmatic perspective throughout this new edition. To do so would have trebled the size of *Rediscover Grammar*. But there is a separate reason: this new perspective is so important, and requires such detailed illustration, that it warrants independent treatment, and this I have provided in a companion volume, *Making Sense of Grammar* (2004), which connects with *Rediscover Grammar* chapter by chapter.

For the present edition, I have added two extra sections to the Introduction: one on ethnic variation and the other on the electronic medium. I have added a new chapter (74) on the grammatical character of texts as wholes, which indicates the way in which educational grammatical studies seem to be moving. And I have made a few minor modifications and additions throughout, to reflect some of the developments in terminology which followed the arrival of the UK National Curriculum.

David Crystal
Holyhead, October 2003

Special symbols

In a few places, I give examples of how words or parts of words are pronounced. The pronunciations are shown in a phonetic transcription, and printed in slant brackets (/ /). The following symbols are used:

/i/	as in *Sid*	/t/	as in *tell*	/s/	as in *Sid*
/iː/	as in *see*	/d/	as in *do*	/z/	as in *zoo*
/ai/	as in *my*	/k/	as in *kiss*	/ð/	as in *this*

The use of a strikethrough in a word or sentence means that the usage is not possible in English: ~~a musics~~.

Abbreviations

The initial letters of certain terms are sometimes used to save space. A complete list of these abbreviations is as follows:

A	adverbial
Adj	adjective
C	complement
C_o	object complement
C_s	subject complement
N	noun
O	object
O_d	direct object
O_i	indirect object
S	subject
V	verb

Introduction

What is grammar?

Grammar is the business of taking a language to pieces, to see how it works. Its study has fascinated people for over 2,000 years – since the time of the Ancient Greeks. But from the 1960s onwards, grammar came to be unpopular. People became disenchanted with the narrow-mindedness and rote learning which characterized the prescriptive approach to language study that had been in place since the eighteenth century. They became uncertain about its value, and many schools ceased to teach it, or taught it very selectively.

The topic became controversial. Some argued strongly that the teaching of 'old-style' grammar (along with multiplication tables) would be a solution to the supposed problems of deteriorating standards in modern education. Others, with unhappy memories of their first close encounter with grammatical study, argued equally strongly that to reintroduce grammar in its old form would be a disaster.

Times have changed, and grammar is back – but with a difference. The educational aim today is to place grammar within a frame of reference which demonstrates its relevance to the active and creative tasks of language production and comprehension. Its study is not an end in itself, but a means of developing our awareness of the expressive richness of 'language in use'. In this way, the new era brings into a fresh relationship the contrasting educational linguistic trends of the early and late twentieth century.

I very much welcome this development, for I believe the study of grammar is something that everyone can find fascinating, fruitful, and even entertaining.

Why apologise?

If you have never studied grammar before, you may find this section unnecessary (in which case, continue on p.12). But if you have, then an apology may be in order. For you may well recall your previous encounter with the subject as 'dry', 'boring', and 'pointless' – to cite just three of the many critical adjectives which have been used. It is a sad result of nineteenth-century educational practices that so many people were made to feel like this. The reasons, looking back, are clear enough.

- English grammar was often taught as if it were a dead language, like Latin. Children were made to learn by heart labels for bits of sentences, without ever finding out what the task was intended to do. Vague explanations were given, such as grammar being a 'discipline for the mind'.

- It was claimed that the ability to analyse (or **parse**) sentences would improve the command of spoken and written language. But there was never any clear evidence presented to support this claim. And the existence of many children who were able to parse, yet whose speech and writing continued to be unsatisfactory, rather argued against it.

- The older (or **traditional**) grammars insisted that only certain styles of English were worth studying – notably, the more formal language of the best literature. Informal styles of speech were ignored, or condemned as incorrect. This meant that the language which children used and heard around them received no attention in the grammar lesson. There was no bridge between the grammar of home and school. To many, the subject became unreal and uninspiring.

'Knowing' grammar or 'knowing about' grammar?

Everyone reading these sentences, and understanding them, already knows the grammar of the English language. Even five-year-old children know most of it. We can see this from the way we speak. We put words together in the right order, with the right endings, and only occasionally make a mistake. We have evidently learned the rules, and we recognise when somebody breaks them. It is 'not English' to say *Cat the on a mat sitting was*. Everyone who speaks English **knows** grammar, intuitively and unconsciously.

But not everyone who speaks English **knows about** grammar. 'Knowing about' means being able to talk about what we know. It means being able to describe what we do, when we string words together, and being able to work out what the rules are. It means learning a number of technical terms, and using them in a clear and consistent way. It is a conscious process, and it does not come naturally.

Why, then, study grammar?

- 'Because it's there.' We are constantly curious about the world in which we live, and wish to understand it and (as with mountains) master it. Grammar is no different from any other domain of knowledge, in this respect.

- But more than mountains, language is involved with almost everything we do, as social beings. We cannot live without language. To understand this aspect of our existence would be no mean achievement. And grammar is the fundamental organising principle of language.

12

- Our grammatical ability is quite extraordinary. It is probably the most creative ability we have. There is no limit to what we can say or write — and yet all of this potential is controlled by a finite number of rules. How is this done? How can we describe these rules?

- Nonetheless, our language can let us down. We encounter ambiguity, imprecision, unintelligible speech or writing. To deal with these problems, we need to put grammar under the microscope, and work out what went wrong. This is critical when, as children, we are learning to emulate the standards used by educated adult members of the community.

- Learning about grammar provides a basis for learning other languages. Much of the apparatus we need in order to study English turns out to be of general usefulness. Other languages have clauses, tenses, and adjectives too. And the differences they display will be all the clearer if we have first grasped what is unique to our mother tongue.

- After studying grammar, we should be more alert to the strength, flexibility and variety of our language, and thus be in a better position to use it and to evaluate others' use of it. Whether our own usage in fact improves, as a result, is less predictable. Our **awareness** must improve, but turning that awareness into better practice — by speaking and writing more effectively — requires an additional set of skills (p.34). Even after a course on car mechanics, we can still drive carelessly.

Using this grammar

This book is a simple introduction to English grammar. But it does not stand on its own. I have followed the general approach found in a series of much larger grammars, widely used in colleges and universities, in particular the vast *A Comprehensive Grammar of the English Language* (p.253). By using the general plan and terminology of this series, my aim is to provide an 'easy way in' to the deeper study of the subject, should you wish to continue with it.

Rediscover Grammar can be used in two ways. To begin with, it should be read as an ordinary book, from beginning to end. This will give you a general sense of the grammar as a whole, and of how the material is organised. Then, at a later stage, the book can be used as an outline reference work. Using the contents page or the index, you can dip into the book at any point, to check the meaning of a term or a point of usage, and follow the system of cross-references in any direction. If you find you need more information, it should not then be difficult to find the corresponding sections in the larger grammars, using their contents pages or indexes.

The information in this book, therefore, should be treated in the same way that you might use a dictionary. Just as many houses have a dictionary which can be used to look words up, as occasion demands, so this grammar can be used – to look constructions up. We often encounter questions of style and usage to do with English grammar, and a large number of these are discussed in *Rediscover Grammar.*

Several general topics are also included (pp.18–35), because of their importance in the school curriculum.

Usage

This book describes the basic features of the way grammar is used in English. It deals with a wide range of spoken and written usage, and includes data on formal, informal, regional, literary, and other styles. Several examples are given of how grammatical notions relate to the language we see and hear around us. And I discuss points of grammar which are currently felt to be particularly controversial.

The information is presented objectively. I indicate areas where people need to be careful about informal usage if they wish to avoid criticism. But there is no condemnation of regional or informal usage. I take the view that all varieties of the language have an intrinsic value and interest, while recognising that one of these varieties – formal Standard English – carries more social prestige and has more universal standing than any other. Issues of this kind are presented in the sections marked **Usage**.

Caution

Rediscover Grammar does not hide the fact that some questions of grammatical analysis in English are extremely tricky. The grammar of a language is not a neat, logical, regular phenomenon. There are always exceptions to rules, and sometimes there are so many exceptions that it is awkward deciding what the rule should be. Often a single sentence can be analysed in more than one way. This is an introductory book, so many of these problems are passed over in silence. But in most sections, attention is drawn to difficulties of analysis or terminology under the heading of **Caution**.

Standard English

Since the 1980s, the notion of 'standard' has been prominent in public discussion about the English language. At national level, in several countries (but especially in the UK), it has been at the centre of the debate surrounding the shape of the English school curriculum. At international level, the focus has been on the question of which national standard to use in teaching English as a foreign language. But before sensible decisions can be made about how to introduce Standard English or teach it, we need to be clear about what it actually is.

A national standard

Any definition of Standard English (SE) within an English-speaking country is going to be quite intricate, for it involves several factors.

- SE is a variety of the English used in that country – a distinctive combination of linguistic features with a particular role to play. Many people call it a 'dialect' of English – and so it is, but of a rather special kind, for it has no local base. There is nothing in the grammar and vocabulary of a piece of SE to tell us which part of a country it comes from.

- SE is the variety of English which carries most prestige within a country. 'Prestige' is a social concept; it means that some people have high standing in the eyes of others, whether this derives from social class, material success, political strength, popular acclaim, or educational background. The English that these people choose to use will become the standard within their community.

- The prestige attached to SE is recognised by the adults in the community, and they will recommend SE as a desirable educational target. It is the variety which is used as the norm by the community's leading institutions, such as its government, law courts, and media. It is therefore the variety which is likely to be the most widely disseminated among the public. It will, accordingly, be widely understood – though not by everyone, and with varying comprehension of some of its features (thus motivating the demands of the various movements for 'plain English'). It may or may not be liked.

- Although SE is widely understood, it is not widely produced in speech. This is a very important point. Only a minority of people within a country actually use it when they talk. Most people speak a variety of regional English, or an admixture of standard and regional Englishes, and reserve such labels as 'BBC English' or 'the Queen's English' for what they perceive to be a 'pure' SE. Similarly, when they write – itself a minority activity – the consistent use of SE is required only in certain tasks (such as a letter to a newspaper, but not necessarily to a close friend). More than anywhere else, SE is to be found in print.

- The linguistic features of SE are chiefly matters of grammar and orthography (spelling and punctuation). It is especially important to note that SE is not a matter of pronunciation: SE is spoken in a wide variety of accents (including, of course, any prestige accent a country may have, such as British 'Received Pronunciation').

Using these five features, we may define the Standard English of an English-speaking country as the minority variety (identified chiefly by its grammar and orthography) which carries most prestige and is most widely understood.

A world standard

If we read the newspapers or listen to newscasters around the English-speaking world, we will quickly develop the impression that there is a World Standard English (WSE), acting as a strongly unifying force among the vast range of variation which exists. However, this impression is not entirely correct. A totally uniform, regionally neutral, and unarguably prestigious variety does not yet exist worldwide.

- Each country where English is a first language is aware of its linguistic identity, and is anxious to preserve it from the influence of others. New Zealanders do not want to be Australians; Canadians do not want to be 'Americans'; and 'Americanism' is perceived as a danger signal by usage guardians everywhere (except of course in the USA).

- Countries can be grouped into those which follow American English, those which follow British English, and those (e.g. Canada) where there is a mixture of influences. One of the most noticeable features of this divided usage is spelling. In certain domains, such as computing and medicine, American spellings are becoming widespread (*program, disk, pediatrics*), but we are a long way from uniformity.

- There are many differences in regional vocabulary, such as the terms of local politics, business, culture, and natural history. There is also a certain amount of grammatical difference, especially between British and American English.

- The notion of a 'standard pronunciation' is useful in the international setting of English as a second or foreign language, but here too there is more than one teaching model – chiefly, British 'Received Pronunciation' (UK) and 'General American' (US).

- The question of prestige is not easy to determine, at an international level, because of the different national histories which coexist. Would it be more prestigious for a report from an international body to appear in British or American spelling? Should it refer to *cars* or *automobiles*? What image do its authors wish to convey? Decisions about such matters are made in innumerable contexts every day. It will take time before the world sees a consensus, and only time will tell whether this consensus will display the domination of a present-day variety of English or the development of a new, composite variety.

A tridialectal future

Wherever World Standard English eventually comes from, a new **bidialectism** (the ability to use two dialects of a language) is sure to emerge. And because many people are already bidialectal (knowing their national standard and a regional dialect), the future is likely to be a **tridialectal** one.
- At home or with friends, we will use a variety of English influenced by the dialect of the region where we live.
- Travelling around the country, for work or for tourism, British people (for example) will use British Standard English.
- Travelling around the world, we will talk together using World Standard English.

Speech and writing

The basic distinction between speech and writing is obvious. Speech uses the transmitting medium of 'phonic substance', typically air-pressure movements produced by the vocal organs. Writing uses 'graphic substance', typically marks on a surface made by a hand using an implement. But there is far more involved than this simple physical difference.

Speech and writing take place in very different communicative situations. There are few circumstances where we are faced with a genuine choice between speaking or writing. Normally, whenever two people are in earshot, they speak to each other. Only very special circumstances (such as children passing secret messages in class) warrant our writing down what we wish to 'say'. Conversely, people separated by distance in space or time, and lacking electronic means of communication, have no alternative but to write to each other.

Moreover, the status of the two mediums is not the same. Written formulations are usually required to make spoken agreements legally binding. Historical documents are given a kind of respect which is rarely accorded to speech. And it is written English which provides the standard that society values (p.16).

The following pages list seven important points of difference between speech (S) and writing (W). S1 should be compared with W1, S2 with W2, and so on. In relation to all points, 'writing' is a shorthand for 'writing and reading', and 'speech' is a shorthand for 'speaking and listening'.

The differences between speech and writing

S1 Speech is time-bound, dynamic, transient. It is part of an interaction in which both participants are usually present, and the speaker has a particular addressee (or several addressees) in mind.

W1 Writing is space-bound, static, permanent. It is the result of a situation in which the writer is usually distant from the reader, and often does not know who the reader is going to be.

S2 The spontaneity and speed of most speech exchanges make it difficult to engage in complex advance planning. The pressure to think while talking promotes looser construction, repetition, rephrasing, and comment clauses (p.214). Intonation and pauses divide long utterances into manageable chunks, but sentence boundaries are often unclear (p.39).

W2 Writing allows repeated reading and close analysis, and promotes the development of careful organisation and compact expression, with often intricate sentence structure (p.200). Units of discourse (sentences, paragraphs) are usually easy to identify through punctuation and layout (p.244).

S3 Because participants are typically in face-to-face interaction, they can rely on such cues as facial expression and gesture to aid meaning (feedback). The lexicon of speech is often characteristically vague, using words which refer directly to the situation – **deictic** (pron. /**daik**tik/) expressions, such as *that one, in here, right now*.

W3 Lack of visual contact means that participants cannot rely on context to make their meaning clear; nor is there any immediate feedback. Most writing therefore avoids the use of deictic expressions, which are likely to be ambiguous. Writers must also anticipate the effects of the time-lag between production and reception, and the problems posed by having their language read and interpreted by many recipients in diverse settings.

S4 Unique features of speech include most of the prosody (p.242). The many nuances of intonation, loudness, tempo, rhythm, and other tones of voice cannot be written down with much efficiency.

W4 Unique features of writing include pages, lines, capitalisation, spatial organisation, and several aspects of punctuation (p.244). Only a very few graphic conventions relate to prosody, such as question marks and underlining for emphasis. Several written genres (e.g. timetables, graphs) cannot be read aloud efficiently, but have to be assimilated visually.

S5 Many words and constructions are characteristic of (especially informal) speech. Lengthy coordinate sentences are normal (p.204), and are often of great complexity. Nonsense vocabulary is not usually written, and may have no standard spelling (*whatchamacallit*). Obscenity may be replaced by graphic euphemism (*f****). Slang and grammatical informality, such as contracted forms (p.85), may be frowned upon.

W5 Some words and constructions are characteristic of writing, such as multiple instances of subordination in the same sentence (p.202), elaborately balanced syntactic patterns, and the long sentences found in some legal documents. Certain items of vocabulary are never spoken, such as the longer names of chemical compounds.

S6 Speech is very suited to social or 'phatic' functions, such as passing the time of day, or any situation where casual discourse is desirable. It is also good at expressing social relationships, and personal opinions and attitudes, due to the vast range of nuances which can be expressed by the prosody and accompanying nonverbal features.

W6 Writing is very suited to the recording of facts and the communication of ideas, and to tasks of memory and learning. Written records are easier to keep and scan; tables demonstrate relationships between things; notes and lists provide mnemonics; and text can be read at speeds which suit a person's ability to learn.

S7 There is an opportunity to rethink an utterance while it is in progress (starting again, adding a qualification). However, errors, once spoken, cannot be withdrawn; the speaker must live with the consequences. Interruptions and overlapping speech are normal and highly audible.

W7 Errors and other perceived inadequacies in our writing can be eliminated in later drafts without the reader ever knowing they were there. Interruptions, if they have occurred while writing, are also invisible in the final product.

Several of these differences are trends rather than absolute distinctions. For example, while a great deal of speech depends on a shared context, and thus uses many situation-dependent expressions (such as *this/that*, *here/there*), it is not true of all speech. A spoken lecture is usually quite self-contained, except when it refers to such things as handouts. On the other hand, such written material as personal letters regularly depends on shared knowledge, and makes use of these expressions. The language thus provides a 'pool' of resources which are used by spoken and written genres in various ways.

The electronic medium

During the 1990s, electronic communication became a daily opportunity for millions through the use of computers and mobile phones (cellphones, in the USA). Immediately, the language began to change, as people devised innovative forms of expression to exploit the strengths and circumvent the weaknesses of the new technology. Within only a decade it was possible to see, in emails, chatroom interactions, Web pages, and text messages, multiple effects on language structure and use as people realized the potential of the medium.

There is no universally agreed name for this medium, though 'computer-mediated communication (CMC)' and 'electronic discourse' are quite widely used. For brevity, I use **Netspeak** for the kind of language observed on the Internet and other networks, and **Textspeak** for that observed in mobile phone interaction. The name is not so important. What needs to be emphasized is that electronic technology has given us a new form of communication. Netspeak and Textspeak are neither varieties of speech nor varieties of writing, but a novel amalgam of the two, offering expressive possibilities which the traditional mediums could never have provided.

Netspeak/Textspeak are not like speech

Most of the differences relate to S1, S3, S4, and S7 on pp.21–3.

- There is no face-to-face interaction, and therefore no simultaneous feedback, overlapping speech, or interruption. We have to wait (sometimes for quite a while) before we receive a reaction from an addressee, and we may never get one.

- Keyboard restrictions disallow the expression of intonation and other dynamic features of speech. Although primitive attempts have been made using smileys (emoticons) such as :) to express attitudes conveyed by prosody and the face, their expressive potential is very limited, they are ambiguous, and they are not widely used.

- Chatroom technology allows us to converse with many addressees at the same time, by reacting individually and in quick succession to the messages of other people. This multidirectional facility is not something we can do in the 'real' speech world.

Netspeak/Textspeak are not like writing

Most of the differences relate to W1, W4, W5, and W7 on pp. 21–3.

- The animacy of the Web has no correlate in traditional writing. Pages can vary in front of your eyes, changing colour, altering text (as with incoming news headlines), and presenting new material (as in pop-up advertising). Writing is no longer intrinsically static or permanent.

- We can respond to incoming emails by breaking up the message into chunks and inserting our reactions at various places (the technique is called 'framing'). There is nothing like this in traditional writing.

- With personal messaging, the time-lag between sending and receiving is typically much shorter than in traditional written interaction, and can be immediate.

- The need for speedy interaction has led to a far greater level of informality, with many of the conventions of Standard English adapted or dropped. In particular, users can avoid punctuation and capitalization, and use nonstandard spellings and abbreviations, without sanction. New conventions have evolved, such as the rebus (C U = 'see you'), the emphatic asterisk (a * big * deal), and the multiple use of punctuation marks or letters (Noooooooo!!!!!).

- Speed and informality combine in person-to-person interaction to make sentences short and loosely constructed. Sentences and paragraphs in the columns and text-blocks of well-designed Web pages also tend to be short (p.237). Considerable use is made there of the minor sentences typical of journalism (p.42). The interactive nature of the medium results in far more question-forms than in traditional written varieties.

Electronic communication is closer to writing than to speech; but the novel opportunities provided by the technology demand that it be treated as an independent medium (see further, p.236). Its idiosyncrasies have no purpose in contexts where the same range of technological constraints on time and space do not operate. The use of Netspeak or Textspeak conventions in formal writing has no possible motivation, and it would be a sign of an immature stylistic sense if a writer were to use them there, other than for a special literary effect.

Varieties of English

The constructions described in this book for the most part identify a 'common core' of English grammar – features which will be found in virtually every situation where the language is used. However, it would be wrong to conclude that there is no systematic grammatical variation in English. Although grammar is the least noticeable dimension of language variation, several constructions have been affected by regional, social, or historical change, and many varieties are distinguished stylistically by the frequency with which particular grammatical features are used.

Regional variation

Regional variations tell us about the geographical origins of the language user, and are of two kinds.

International   These features signal global identities, such as the contrasts which distinguish British and American English, or Caribbean, Indian, and West African varieties of English (see further, p.29).

Intranational   These features signal identities within a country, such as the contrasts which distinguish Scots, Irish, and Welsh English, or Northern, Liverpudlian, and West Country varieties of British English.

* Narrower distinctions can be drawn, so that often different areas within a state, county, or city can be identified – as in the Bronx accent heard in New York City.

Intranational varieties are the ones which are usually called dialects, though this term can equally be used for international varieties also. We would then have to refer to 'British English' as a dialect of 'World English'.

Caution

Regional variation is not a stable phenomenon. Dialects are always changing, and influence each other in sometimes unpredictable ways. Patterns of American English, in particular, have for some time been influencing the speech of people in other parts of the world, and several of the **Usage** issues identified in this book have come about for this reason.

Not everyone likes it when they notice the emergence of different grammatical patterns from the ones they have themselves used since childhood. Some people get angry, condemn the changes, and protest about them to anyone who will listen. Change is invariably considered to be for the worse. But no one has ever managed to stop the course of grammatical change, as can be seen from the way. English grammar has steadily evolved over the centuries.

Some aspects of grammar are particularly susceptible to regional variation. In English, it is the verb phrase which is most often affected, especially those features involved in the expression of time, such as auxiliary verbs (pp.86–8) and tense endings (p.80). Pronouns, too, are often distinctive (p.161).

- In answer to a *have* question (p.87) (*Do you have a five-pound note?*), British English prefers to repeat the *have* (*Yes, I have*), whereas American English prefers to substitute *do* (*Yes, I do*).

- Contracted forms (p.86) with the auxiliary verb shortened (*she's not, I've not*) will be heard in some areas (e.g. Scotland, England); in others it is the negative word which is shortened (*she isn't, I haven't*).

- Second-person pronouns (p.161) display particular variation: *youse* (Ireland, Liverpool, Glasgow, northern USA), *y'all* (southern USA), *thou/thee* (parts of rural England), and *ye* (Ireland, Scotland) are among the commonly used forms.

Some other regional grammatical variants are mentioned later in the book, in relation to sentence tags (p.51), past tenses (pp.80, 105), the subjunctive (p.94), spelling (p.95), adverb suffixes (p.175), prepositions (p.191), and inversion (p.227).

The English Dialect Survey (of locations in rural England) has recorded all the following ways of varying the phrase *'m not*. Some are no more than variant pronunciations, but several involve quite different grammatical rules from those found in Standard English, such as the use of *be* or *is* after the first-person pronoun.

ain't, amment, amn', aren't, ammet, amno', baan't, bain't, ben't, binno', bisn't, byen't, byun't, en't, in't, isn't, 'm none, 're not, 's not, yen't, yun't

---

Ethnic variation

The growing multicultural composition of present-day society has made more noticeable grammatical features of identity which reflect divergent ethnic origins. These features do more than simply signal regional background: they also act as markers of belonging to a particular cultural group. They are not part of the standard language, and are rarely encountered in public writing, other than in literary work.

In the past, these features were ridiculed in the street and playground as an easy target by those unable to cope with cultural diversity, and such linguistic antagonism is regrettably still encountered. They were also often penalized in the classroom by teachers unable to free themselves from the blinkers of two centuries of a prescriptive tradition (p.11) in which Standard English was the only permitted focus of attention. Thanks to a more egalitarian attitude present in schools, in which language variety is appreciated as an intrinsic good, part of the expressive richness of a language, ethnic dialects now tend to be explored for what they add to the language mix found in most classrooms.

We have come to appreciate the irony of, on the one hand, trying to inculcate positive attitudes towards language and language use (in the form of Standard English) while on the other hand making children feel inferior by pouring scorn on the regional or ethnic dialect which comes most naturally to them. Present-day language policy aims to appreciate all varieties for what they are – expressions of regional and cultural identity – while acknowledging that one variety, Standard English, has an especially important role in defining our status as educated, outward-looking individuals.

Some Caribbean features

The English spoken by people of Caribbean origin provides an example of distinctive grammatical identity, which is often encountered in contemporary poetry and prose. A wide range of syntactic and morphological features (p.241) is found, but we should note that there is considerable variation among the islands of the Caribbean, and a further dimension of variation when we encounter dialects which have evolved in other places, such as the UK.

- Lack of concord between subject and verb in the present tense (p.74): *She sing in the school choir.*
- There are no forms of *be* as a copula (p.64) or auxiliary (p.84): *They too hot to eat, They going on the bus.*
- Adjectives are routinely used in adverbial function (p.174): *They done it good.*
- Variable nouns (p.122) often have no plural ending: *We go in two car.*
- The *'s* ending expressing the genitive relationship (p.132) is often omitted: *My sister book on the floor.*
- Pronouns tend not to show case distinctions (p.155): *He take he coat, Her go to school.*
- Past tenses can be expressed using the base form of the verb without an ending, or by some other form (p.100): *We go to the club last night, We been see the film.*
- Did is often used as a past tense marker with stative verbs (p.107): *They did know the answer.*
- Completed action (p.104) is expressed by *done*: *I just done washed the car.*
- Auxiliary *do* is not used in question forms (p.84): *How you get that?*

Historical variation

There have been many changes in English grammar over the past thousand years. There is no space to describe them in this little book, but it is worth pointing out that, for anyone who does wish to investigate earlier periods from a grammatical point of view, it is possible to make use of the same grammatical apparatus that is presented here. For example, what are usually said to be changes in 'word order' between Old and Middle English (more precisely, changes in the order of clause elements) can be described with reference to the categories explained on pp.44–5.

A few points of ongoing grammatical change are mentioned at various places in the book, such as in relation to auxiliary verbs (pp.86–7), gender (pp.164–5), and punctuation (p.135), and there is the occasional reference to archaism (pp.86, 161). Most of the points discussed under the heading of **Usage** turn out to be matters of grammatical change.

Stylistic variation

Under this heading is included a wide range of variation, relating to such matters as the formality of the situation, the specialised nature of the discourse, and the intentions of the speaker or writer. In particular, the distinction between informal and formal style has many consequences for the study of grammar.

- There are numerous differences in formal and informal sentence construction (e.g. pp.39, 207, 214, 221, 227). Some of these are well-known points of disputed usage, such as the placement of a preposition within a sentence (p.195).

- Differences in word structure can convey varying levels of formality, such as the choice between *who* and *whom* (p.149), subjective and objective pronouns (p.66), or foreign and native plurals (p.123).

- Several specific constructions are associated with informal speech and writing, such as the use of *got* (p.87), *gotta* (p.89), *get* (p.98), and *gonna* (*going to,* p.108). Contracted forms, abbreviated clauses, and tags are also characteristic of informality (pp.51, 53, 54, 199, 227). Correspondingly, several forms are associated with formality, such as the subjunctive (p.93), *may* (p.111), and subordination (p.209).

Professional varieties

The style we associate with occupations is often identified by the frequency of certain grammatical constructions.

- Newspapers, advertisements, radio news summaries and other attention-grabbing contexts make frequent use of minor sentences (p.43), adjective sequences (p.115), and inversions of word order (p.221).
- Varieties where objectivity is critical, such as scientific English, motivate the use of the passive construction (p.99), which is the chief means of expressing an impersonal point of view.
- The traditions of religious English promote the retention of archaic grammatical features, such as the use of *O* (p.72) and *thou* (p.161)

  Longer examples from two varieties are analysed on pp.232–7.

Grammar and other areas

The study of grammar should never be divorced from the study of meaning (**semantics**), or from the study of the effects achieved when grammatical constructions are used in real situations (**pragmatics**).

Semantics

Every grammatical construction has a function, or meaning – though often it is one which can be described only in an abstract way.

* The contrast between active and passive verb phrases (p.96) makes available a choice between personal and impersonal expression: *Mary poured the mixture into the jar* vs. *The mixture was poured into the jar.*

* Determiners (p.136) allow us to express many distinctions of quantity, definiteness, and possession: *the, some, this, my, enough, every.*

* Auxiliary verbs (pp.84, 110) convey, or help to convey, such notions as time, frequency, obligation, possibility, and necessity: *may, will, must.*

* Pronouns (p.154) express various gender possibilities, chiefly male vs. female, but also personal vs. impersonal, one vs. many, ownership, and distance: *he, she, one, they, my, that.*

* Conjunctions (p.212) and prepositions (p.192) express a wide range of notions, such as time, place, reason, and concession: *before, on, to, at, because.*

Most sections of this book present grammatical rules – abstract statements (such as S + V + O, p.46) which apply to many instances. But quite often, in the study of grammar, we find ourselves talking about the properties of an **individual** word or phrase.

We can see this happening when we describe the different irregular nouns (p.123) and verbs (p.81), pronouns (pp.156, 160), auxiliary verbs (pp.84, 88, 108, 110), and the idiosyncratic forms which play a part in the noun phrase, such as the articles (p.138) and the words which go with them (pp.140, 142). There will be specific things to say about such items as *let* (p.53), *what* and *how* (p.54), *none* (p.75), *more* and *most* (p.172), *please* (p.182), *than* (p.216), and *there* (p.227).

Pragmatics

The use of some grammatical constructions is closely bound up with the assumptions and social conventions which people bear in mind when they talk or write to each other. For example, the use of the vocative construction (p.72) is largely governed by social constraints, as is the use of first names (p.73), modal verbs (p.110), and personal pronouns (p.161). The order in which you say things alters what you want your listener to attend to (pp.223–7). And how much you leave out of a sentence (p.198) depends on what you assume your listener already knows. Semantic and pragmatic issues are the focus of *Making Sense of Grammar* (p.253).

The aim of a grammar is to describe the way a language's **sentences** are constructed. Everyone uses the concept of 'sentence'. We imagine we speak in sentences, and we teach children to write in them, making sure they put in all the full stops. But in fact sentences are not easy to define.

Many people remember the old definition of a sentence: 'a complete expression of a single thought'. Unfortunately, this **notional** approach is too vague to be helpful.

- There are many sentences which seem to express a single thought, but which are not complete:

  Beautiful day!   Nice one, Cyril.   Taxi!

- There are many sentences which are complete, but express more than one thought:

  For his birthday, Freddy wants a bike, a robot, a car, and a visit to the cinema.

The alternative approach begins by describing the way sentences are constructed – the patterns of words they contain. This is the **formal** approach to English grammar.

Three general points apply to any English sentence.

- It is constructed according to a system of rules, known by all the adult mother-tongue speakers of the language. A sentence formed in this way is said to be grammatical.

- It is a construction which can be used on its own, without people feeling that it is incomplete.

- It is the largest construction to which the rules of grammar apply. (The formation of larger units, such as paragraphs, is discussed on p.228.)

This book explains the rules of English grammar, and by so doing defines the structure and use of sentences.

Grammatical, ungrammatical – and others

- The following are all possible sentences, which everyone would automatically accept.

  The dentist has written to you again.   Come in.
  Where have you been?

- The following are not possible sentences (they are **ungrammatical**, shown by the strikethrough):

  ~~The of a car is.~~   ~~What and why did he go?~~

- And there are some problems. Shall we call these sentences grammatical?

  At the airport.   I ain't doing nothing!   Damn!
  I want you to boldly go somewhere. (p.177)

Usage

A sentence is something which begins with a capital letter and ends with a full stop? This definition, which applies only to the written language, is faulty on three counts:

- We have to allow for question marks and exclamation marks as well (see the first sentence on this page).

- Punctuation is often not used, and yet we still know that the construction is a sentence. Many advertisements, public notices, newspaper headlines, and legal documents lack punctuation marks.

Bush urges separate deal

The next time you have business with the Vikings fly direct with the Danish Airline

- People disagree about the best way to punctuate a text. Some manuals of style say you should never end a sentence before such words as *and* or *but* (see p.204), and this rule is often taught in schools. But there are other manuals which accept that authors often do begin sentences in this way (usually to emphasise a contrast in meaning), and these do not condemn the usage. There are illustrious precedents. In this extract, both rules are in operation:

> There were gentlemen and there were seamen in the navy of Charles the Second. But the seamen were not gentlemen; and the gentlemen were not seamen.
>
> (*History of England,* Thomas Macaulay)

Caution

It is **much** more difficult to identify sentences in natural spoken conversation. Words like *and* are frequently used, making it difficult for a grammarian to work out where one sentence ends and the next begins.

Transcribing spontaneous speech

As this is speech, there are no capital letters. Pauses are shown by –; units of rhythm by /.

well when the children fed the pigs / they all had to stand well back / – and they were allowed to take the buckets / – but they weren't allowed to get near the pigs / you see / – so they weren't very happy …

This kind of loosely structured utterance is normal and inevitable. People sometimes hotly deny that they would speak in such a way – but a home tape-recording of an informal conversation quickly shows that they do.

This should not be surprising. In situations where we have to speak spontaneously, there is no time to plan far ahead, to work out where the 'full stops' ought to go. Spoken sentences therefore have a very different kind of structure from written sentences.

Types of sentence

It is obvious, as we look through the pages of a novel, or a daily newspaper, that there must be a very large number of sentence patterns in English. What is less obvious is that these can be grouped into two main types, on the basis of whether they are formed in a **regular** or **irregular** way. Regular sentences are often referred to as **major**; irregular sentences as **minor**.

Major sentences

Major sentences are in the vast majority. All the sentences in this book (apart from the headings, and a few of the examples) are of this type. Essentially, they are sentences which can be broken down into a specific pattern of elements, such as these:

My wife	has dropped	a book	on her foot.
I	gave	the keys	to Luke.
Jemima	went	to town	yesterday.

Clauses

The phrase 'specific pattern of elements' is awkward. Instead, many grammars use the term **clause**. We shall see what can be a clause, and what to call its elements, on p.44.

Simple and multiple sentences

Consider the difference between these two sentences:

A book has fallen on John's foot.
A book has fallen on John's foot and a book has fallen on
   Mary's foot.

The same clause pattern turns up twice in the second sentence
(apart from the change of name). Indeed, it is possible to
imagine a sentence in which this clause pattern is used
repeatedly, with innumerable books falling on innumerable feet,
and just the name changing each time. As long as the speaker
kept adding *and* ... *and* ... *and* ..., or some other linking word,
the sentence could continue indefinitely.

Sentences, then, may consist of just one clause, or more than
one clause. A one-clause sentence is called a **simple** sentence.
A sentence which can be immediately analysed into more than
one clause is called a **multiple** sentence. The difference can be
summarised in a diagram:

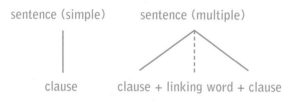

Multiple sentences are described further on p.200. In this first
part of the grammar, all the examples will be of simple
sentences.

2

Minor sentences

Minor sentences are not constructed in a regular way. They use abnormal patterns which cannot be clearly analysed into a sequence of clause elements, as major sentences can. There are only a few minor sentence types, but instances of each type are frequently used in everyday conversation and when conversations are represented in fiction.

Some minor sentence types

- Formulae for stereotyped social situations.

  Hello.   How do you do?   Thanks.   Cheers!

- Emotional noises (known as interjections).

  Eh?   Hey!   Tut-tut.   Ugh!   Ow!   Shhh!

- Proverbs or pithy sayings (aphorisms).

  Easy come, easy go.   Like father, like son.

- Abbreviated forms, such as are used in postcards, instructions, or commentaries.

  Wish you were here.   Mix well.   One lap more.

- Words and phrases (p.114) used as exclamations, questions, or commands.

  Nice day!   Oh for a gin!   Taxi?   All aboard!

Minor sentences do not follow all the rules of English grammar. For example, in a major sentence, verbs can change their tenses from present to past (p.100):

How do you manage? →
How did you manage?

But the greeting *How do you do?* is a minor sentence. We cannot change its tense, and say *How did you do?* Nor can we change the pronoun (p.154) and ask *How does he do?* The sentence has to be learned as a whole, and used as an idiom.

FOR SALE

NO SMOKING

THE TIMES

EXIT

Minor sentences are common in notices, headlines, labels, advertisements, sub-headings, and other kinds of written language where a message is presented as a 'block'.

Caution

Some types of minor sentence look quite complex, and might be confused with a major pattern. But in each case there is something 'odd' about them. For example, one type uses archaic forms (the 'subjunctive', p.93) to express wishes. Another uses question words idiomatically.

God **save** the Queen!   Lord **forbid**!
How about a lift?   **How come** he's not here?

3

Clause elements

All clauses are made up out of **elements**, each expressing a particular kind of meaning. There are just five types of clause element. All five appear in this sentence:

The attendant / has called / me / a fool / twice.

* The first element in this sentence is the **subject (S)**. The subject usually identifies the theme or topic of the clause. Subjects are described on p.60.

* The second element is the **verb (V)**. The verb expresses a wide range of meanings, such as actions, sensations, or states of being. Verbs are described on p.56.

* The third element is the **object (O)**. Objects identify who or what has been directly affected by the action of the verb. The main types of object are described on p.62.

* The fourth element is the **complement (C)**. Complements give further information about another clause element. In the above sentence, *a fool* adds to the meaning of *me*. The main types of complement are described on p.64.

* The fifth element is the **adverbial (A)**. Adverbials usually add information about the situation, such as the time of an action, or (as in the above sentence) its frequency. Other adverbial roles are described on p.68.

In 90% of clauses containing a subject, verb, and object, the subject precedes the verb, and the verb precedes the object. The main exceptions are described on p.49 and p.224.

Caution

- A clause element is not the same as a word. An element may be a single word, or several words. These sentences contain a subject, verb, and object, but there are varying numbers of words:

Subject	Verb	Object
I	planted	a flower.
All the kids	have eaten	chocolate.

- In multiple sentences (p.200), some clause elements can consist of a **whole clause**. Notice how, in the following sentences, the object always answers the question 'What did he say?':

He said yes.   He said a prayer.
He said that he was ready.

That he was ready is a clause (a 'subordinate' clause, p.210), here acting as object of *said*.

Clause elements combine into a very small number of patterns. In fact, most sentences can be analysed into one of only **seven** basic clause types. (A few exceptional cases are described later, see pp.52, 168, 198, 224.) Each type consists of two, three, or four elements.

The seven basic clause types

S: subject, V: verb, O: object, C: complement, A: adverbial

- **S + V**   Hilary / yawned.

- **S + V + O**   Hilary / opened / the door.

- **S + V + C**   Hilary / is / ready.

- **S + V + A**   Hilary / lives / in London.

- **S + V + O + O**   Hilary / gave / me / a pen.

- **S + V + O + C**   Hilary / got / a shoe / wet.

- **S + V + O + A**   Hilary / put / the box / on the table.

The clause elements are sometimes used in a different sequence. This especially happens with questions (p.49), but certain variations are also possible with statements. Notice, for example, how emphatic a sentence becomes when an element which normally occurs towards the end of the clause is placed at the beginning (p.224).

Emerick Royston Freetitle / his name / is!
C   **S**   **V**

Caution

The adverbial element is different from the others, as it can be used often in a clause.

I / leaned / on the stick / again / happily.
S **V**   **A**   **A**   **A**

The first of these As is **obligatory**. *I leaned* needs another element to be complete, and this is provided by *on the stick*. The other As in this sentence are **optional**, giving extra information about time and manner. They can be left out, and the sentence is still grammatical.

Sometimes, **all** the As in a clause are optional. The sentence *Then I laughed loudly* is **A** + **S** + **V** + **A**, but the two As could be omitted, to leave the grammatical sentence *I laughed*. Parentheses can be used to show that an element is optional: **(A) SV (A)**.

Statements and questions

Statements

All the clause types illustrated on p.46 are statements. A statement is a sentence whose purpose is primarily to convey information. Two criteria usually apply:

- The clause contains a subject.

- The subject precedes the verb.

Such sentences are said to have a **declarative** structure.

Caution

- In conversation, the subject is often omitted from a declarative sentence:

  Beg pardon.   Told you so.   Looks like rain.

- In a very few cases, the subject follows a verb. This happens when the clause is introduced by such words as *hardly* and *scarcely*, which express a negative meaning:

  Hardly **had he** left, when the heavens opened.

Questions

Questions are sentences which seek information. They fall into three main types, depending on the kind of reply they expect, and on how they are constructed. Sentences formed in these ways are said to have an **interrogative** structure.

- **Yes–no questions** allow an affirmative or negative reply, often just *yes* or *no*. The subject follows a verb (the 'auxiliary', p.84).

  Will Michael resign?   Are they ready?

- **Wh- questions** allow a reply from a wide range of possibilities. They begin with a question word, such as *what, why, where,* or *how.*

  Where are you going?   Why didn't he answer?

- **Alternative questions** require a reply which relates to the options given in the sentence. They always contain the connecting word *or.*

  Will you travel by train or by boat?

Caution

A questioning tone of voice (p.242) can turn a statement into a yes–no question. Such questions have the structure of a declarative sentence. The tone of voice has become particularly common, especially among young people, in recent decades.

Mary's outside?   You've spoken to her?

Tag questions

Sometimes the interrogative structure is left to the end of the sentence, in the form of a **tag question**.

It's there, **isn't it**?   She's not in, **is she**?

Tag questions also expect the reply *yes* or *no*.

Exclamatory questions

Some sentences resemble questions in their structure, but are used as exclamations (p.54). They express the speaker's strong feelings, and ask the hearer to agree.

Hasn't she grown!   Wasn't the book marvellous!

Often, both positive and negative forms of the sentence can be used, with very little difference in meaning.

Wasn't he angry!   Was he angry! (I'll say he was!)

Rhetorical questions

These sentences also resemble questions in their structure, but they are used as if they were emphatic statements. The speaker does not expect an answer.

Who cares? How should I know? What difference does it make?

'Whose questions are you calling rhetorical?'

- The *-n't* ending of a tag question is replaced by *not* in formal English. In legal cross-examination one might hear:

They left early, did they not?

This usage is conversationally normal in some regional dialects, such as northern British and Irish.

- Informal English uses a few words (e.g. *eh?*, *OK?* and *right?*) which perform the same function as tag questions.

You'll be there in the afternoon, right?

Dialects often make distinctive use of these words, such as in Canada (*eh?*), London (*right?*), and Wales (*ay?*).

Caution

If we change the intonation (p.242), we alter the meaning of a tag question. When the melody is rising, the sentence is 'asking'; when it is falling, the sentence is 'telling'. In writing, the punctuation can indicate the difference:

She's not in, is she? (I really want to know)
She's not in, is she! (I told you so)

But in speech this contrast can be unclear, prompting the complaint 'Are you asking me, or telling me?'

Directives are sentences which instruct someone to do something. They are often called **commands**, but this term is somewhat misleading. Commanding is just one of the many uses of directive sentences.

Some uses of directive sentences

- **Commanding**   Sit down immediately!

- **Inviting**   Have a drink with me tonight.

- **Warning**   Mind your head on the beam.

- **Pleading**   Help me!

- **Advising**   Take an aspirin.

- **Requesting**   Open the window, please.

- **Expressing good wishes**   Have a nice day!

In each case, the verb is in its basic form, with no endings (p.78), and there is usually no subject element present. Structures of this type are called **imperatives**. Directive sentences typically have an imperative structure.

Different kinds of directives

Some directives do not use the basic pattern.

- They allow a subject, with a strong stress.

  You be quiet!   Nobody move!   Everyone go!

- They begin with *let*, followed by a subject.

  Let me see.   Let us pray.   Let's go.

- They begin with *do* or *don't*.

  Do come in.   Don't laugh.   Do not answer.

Usage

- *Let us* is often colloquially abbreviated to *Let's*.

- *Let* with a subject in the third person (p.160) is very formal, and elevates the tone of the proceedings.

  Let no one think that grammar is dull.

Caution

Let as a directive is a different verb from *let* meaning 'permit'. *Let us go* (= 'shall we go?') differs grammatically from *Let us go* (= 'free us'). Only the first can be changed to *Let's go*.

Exclamations

Exclamations are sentences whose main role is to express the extent to which speakers are impressed or aroused by something. They often take the form of a single word or short phrase – a minor sentence (p.42) such as *Gosh!*, *Oh dear*, or *Of all the cheek!*. But exclamations can also have a major sentence structure.

- Their first element begins with *what* or *how*, and is followed by a subject and verb, in that order:

  What a lovely day it is! What a mess you've made!
  How nice she looks!   How I used to hate grammar!

- They also occur frequently in a reduced (or 'elliptical', p.198) form, using only the first element:

  What a lovely day! How nice! What a mess!

Both types are said to have an **exclamative** structure.

Exclamatives with subject and verb inverted are very rare. They can sometimes be found in literary English:

How often **have I** cursed that terrible day!

Echo utterances

The traditional classification of major sentences recognises **statements**, **questions**, **commands** (here called **directives**), and **exclamations**. But there is a fifth type of sentence, used only in dialogue, whose function is to confirm, question, or clarify what the previous speaker has just said. This is the **echo utterance.**

Echo utterance structure reflects that of the preceding sentence, which it repeats in whole or in part. All types of sentence can be echoed.

- **Statements** A: John didn't like the film.
                 B: He didn't what?

- **Questions** A: Have you got my knife?
                 B: Have I got your wife?!

- **Directives** A: Sit down here.
                 B: Down there?

- **Exclamations** A: What a lovely day!
                 B: What a lovely day, indeed!

Usage

Echoes sometimes sound impolite unless accompanied by an apologetic 'softening' phrase, such as *I'm sorry* or *I beg your pardon*. This is most noticeable with the question *What did you say?*, often shortened to *What?*. 'Don't say *what*, say *pardon*' is a common parental plea to children.

The verb element plays a central role in clause structure. It is the most **obligatory** of all the clause elements, as can be seen from such clauses as

That old farmer drinks beer by the bucketful.
  S   **V**   **O**   **A**

where other elements can be omitted – but not the verb.

We can omit:

* The adverbial: That old farmer drinks beer.

* The object: That old farmer drinks by the bucketful.

* The subject, in casual style: Drinks beer by the bucketful. (nodding in his direction)

But we cannot omit the verb: ~~That old farmer beer by the bucketful.~~

The verb is a predictable, dependable element of clause structure – with just one kind of exception (the 'verbless' clauses, illustrated on p.168).

What can be a verb element?

Only a verb or verb phrase (p.76):

Run! The bus **is coming**.
The boys **have been eating** crisps.
I **haven't got** any. I'm sorry.

Caution

Note that in this approach the word **verb** is used to refer to the clause element **as a whole** as well as to the words that can be used **within** that element. The difference can be shown as follows:

Charles went home. Charles has gone home.
 S V A   S V A
  verb   verb verb

In the first sentence, the **verb element** (given a capital 'V') consists of just one **verb** (written with a small 'v'). In the second sentence, the V element consists of two verbs.

The second sentence is not to be analysed as **S + V + V + A**. Only **one** V element is allowed per clause. This is because the sequence of verbs is seen as working together to express a single meaning (here, past time).

Some approaches to grammar distinguish the two senses of 'verb' by different terms – for example, calling the Verb a Predicator.

Transitive and intransitive

The choice of the verb actually determines, to a large extent, what other elements can be used in the clause. Once we have 'picked' our verb, certain other things are likely to happen.

- If we pick *go*, we can stop the clause there, without fear of being ungrammatical:

That farmer's going.

Verbs of this type, which can be used without an object, have long been called **intransitive** verbs.

Some common intransitive verbs

appear	die	digress	fall	go
happen	lie	matter	rise	wait

- If we pick *enjoy*, another element has to follow. We cannot say ~~That farmer's enjoying.~~ It has to be *That farmer's enjoying his drink*, with the object present.

Verbs which require an object are traditionally known as **transitive** verbs.

Some common transitive verbs

bring	carry	desire	find	get
keep	like	make	need	use

Uses of verbs

Some grammarians prefer to talk about transitive or intransitive **uses** of verbs. This is because many verbs can be used in either way, to express different meanings. Compare the following:

She's expecting a reply.   She's expecting.
He worked wonders.   He worked.

A few verbs can be transitive or intransitive **without** a change of meaning: compare *I'm eating cake* and *I'm eating*.

> The test for transitivity is to try the verb with various objects. If the sentences are possible, the verb is being used transitively. If not, it is being used intransitively.

Caution

Beware **idioms**. A verb which is transitive in most uses may appear intransitively in an idiom – or vice versa. *Say* and *mean* are usually transitive (*I say so, I mean it*), but not here:

I **say**! Look what Mervyn's wearing!
It wasn't my fault. I **mean** – really!

Similarly, **go** is usually intransitive – but not in the sentence *Will the dog go the course?*.

The subject element

Several criteria combine to identify the **subject** of a clause.

- The subject usually appears before the verb in statements, and after the first verb in questions (p.49):

  Rain fell steadily.   Are **you** going far?

- The subject controls whether the verb is singular or plural in the third person of the present tense (p.100):

  She sees you.   **They see** you.

- The subject also controls the form of certain objects and complements:

  I shaved **my**self.   **He** shaved **him**self.
  They shaved **them**selves.
  Jim's my **friend**.   **Joe and Jim** are my **friends**.

- Some pronouns (p.160) have a distinctive form when used as subjects (the **subjective** form):

  I can see him.   **He** can see me.

What can be a subject?

- Noun phrases, including single nouns (p.112):

  Bob passed out.   **The train** was late.
  Beer, crisps and cheese are on offer.

- Pronouns (p.154):

  I like snails. **That** intrigues me.
  Who did that?   (cf. **He** did that.)

- Some subordinate clauses (p.208):

  What she said was funny. (cf. **It** was funny.)
  Where you live isn't important. (cf. **It** isn't important.)

Caution

Sometimes nouns are used in a series, linked by commas (in writing), by intonation (in speech), or by words like *and*. In these cases, the whole series is analysed as a **single** subject element, and not as a series of different subjects.

Jim, Brian, and Fred were drunk.
     S   **V**   **C**

This is not analysed **S** + **S** + **S** + **V** + **C**, in this approach. There is only one subject per clause.

Object elements usually follow the subject and verb in a clause. Two types of object can be distinguished: **direct** and **indirect**.

- The direct object (O_d) typically refers to some person or thing directly affected by the action expressed by the verb:

  The little boy smashed **a window**.   I saw **Mary**.
     S   V O_d S V O_d

- The indirect object (O_i) typically refers to an animate being that is the recipient of the action. In these cases, a direct object is usually present in the clause as well:

  She gave **the dog** a stroke.   I told **him** my news.
   S V O_i O_d S V O_i O_d

  Notice that the indirect object **precedes** the direct object in these constructions.

Some pronouns (p.160) have a distinctive form when used as objects (the **objective** form):

I saw **him**.   He gave **me** the key.

What can be an object?

- Noun phrases, including single nouns (p.112):

  I saw **Fred**.   We've found **a new house**.

- Pronouns (p.154):

  Fred saw **me**.   Now hear **this**.   He did **what**?

- Some subordinate clauses (p.208):

  She said **I'd been foolish**.   (cf. She said **this**.)

An indirect object can be changed into a corresponding prepositional phrase (p.188). In such cases, **O$_i$** is usually placed **after O$_d$**.

I gave Sam a pen. → I gave a pen to Sam.

Caution

- If there is only one object in the clause, this is usually the direct object. However, with a few verbs, the indirect object can be used alone. *You pay me the rest* can give either *You pay me* or *You pay the rest*.

- As with subjects (p.60), a set of connected noun phrases is analysed as a **single** element. *He / saw / a cat, a dog and a cow* is **S + V + O**.

11 The complement element

The complement element expresses a meaning which adds to that of another clause element – either the subject (the **subject complement**) or the object (the **object complement**).

- A subject complement (**C$_s$**) usually follows the subject and verb. The verb is most often a form of *be* (*is, was*, etc.), but it may also be one of several other verbs that are able to link the complement meaning with the subject meaning. These are called **copular** (or 'linking') verbs.

He is **a doctor**.
The bull became **angry**. (i.e. It **was** angry.)
That tune sounds **marvellous**. (i.e. It **is** marvellous.)

Some copular verbs (with complements)

appear (happy) feel (annoyed) grow (tired)
remain (silent) seem (a fool) turn (cold)

- An object complement (**C$_o$**) usually follows the direct object (p.62), and its meaning relates to that element. The basic identity between them is shown in parentheses.

They elected him **president**. (i.e. He **was** president.)
She made me **angry**. (i.e. I **was** angry.)

What can be a complement?

- Noun phrases, including single nouns (p.112):

  Susan is a **journalist**.   They became **doctors**.

- Adjective phrases, including single adjectives (p.169):

  Arthur is **very happy**.   The car's **ready**.

- Pronouns (p.154):

  This is **him**.   Where's **that**?   That's **who**?

- Some subordinate clauses (p.208):

  That's **what I replied**.   (cf. That's **my reply**.)

When the complement is a noun phrase, it agrees in number (p.74) with its corresponding element.

- A singular subject requires a singular **C$_s$**, and a plural subject requires a plural **C$_s$**.

  The **child** is an **angel**.
  The **children** are **angels**.

- A singular object requires a singular **C$_o$**, and a plural object requires a plural **C$_o$**.

  I find your **child** an **angel**.
  I find your **children angels**.

Usage

Usage varies when the subject complement is a pronoun with both a subjective and an objective form, such as *I/me*.

- In very **formal** contexts, the subjective form is preferred (especially in American English) (p.163).

  That is he.   I am she.

- **Informal** contexts prefer the objective form.

  That's him.   I'm her.

The formal use is often criticised as unidiomatic and stilted. Purists defend such uses as *It is I* on the grounds that Latin required the subjective ('nominative') form after the verb *be*. Critics of this view say that the rules of Latin grammar are not relevant for English.

Caution

Because subject complements and objects both follow the verb, it is important to see the difference between them. The essential point is that there is some identity between the meaning of the complement and that of the subject, whereas there is no such identity between an object and a subject. To say that *Brian became a doctor* (**S** + **V** + **C**) is to say that *Brian is a doctor*. But there is no such implication in *Brian kissed a doctor* (**S** + **V** + **O**).

Clauses

"Excuse me, Bill, but I don't see how 'To be or not to be' could possibly be the question."

Alternative analyses

Some clause structures can be analysed in more than one way, especially when the usage is figurative or idiomatic. For example, is *It costs two pounds* **SVO** or **SVA**?

- **SVO**? Compare *I kicked the ball*. Both sentences answer the question 'What?':

  What did he kick? The ball.
  What did it cost? Two pounds.

- **SVA**? Compare *I care a lot*. Both sentences answer the question 'How much?':

  How much does he care? A lot.
  How much did it cost? Two pounds.

It is not possible to make a definite decision in such cases. *It costs two pounds* seems to combine aspects of both SVO and SVA structures. Other examples include:

  He ran a mile. (**SVO** or **SVA**?)
  She is in good health. (**SVC** or **SVA**?)
  Today will be fine. (**SVC** or **AVC**?)

The **adverbial** differs from the other clause elements in several respects:

- One clause can contain several instances:

  I arrived on the bus / on Thursday / in the rain / wearing a hat / eating grapes / ...

- Adverbials can be used in several possible positions within the clause (though most commonly at the end):

  (Twice) he (twice) asked me (twice).

- Adverbials express a wide range of meanings, such as manner, space, and time (p.178):

  Jim stayed **quietly** / **in bed** / **all day**.
  MANNER   SPACE   TIME

- Adverbials perform several roles in sentence construction. Some add information about an event (*He walked* **quietly**). Some link clauses together (*The bus was full; however, I found a seat*). And some add a comment about what is being expressed (**Frankly**, *I think he's wrong*). These types are described on pp.180–7.

- When adverbials relate specifically to the meaning expressed by the verb, they are said to **modify** the verb.

What can be an adverbial?

- Adverb phrases, including single adverbs (p.175):

  They ran **quickly** – **very quickly**.

- Prepositional phrases (p.188):

  We strolled **in the garden**.

- Some nouns and noun phrases (p.112):

  That girl phoned me **today** – **this morning**.

- Some subordinate clauses (**adverbial clauses**), (p.210):

  The children roared **when they saw the clown**.

Caution

Most adverbials are optional, but a small number of verbs **require** an adverbial to complete their meaning (see the clause types **SVA** and **SVOA** on p. 46). These verbs include the following:

I **put** the book – on the table.
We **live** – in a city.
The path **goes** – around the field.
The play **lasts** – for two hours.
Cannes **lies** – on the Riviera.
The children **kept** – out of trouble.

A **vocative** refers to the person or persons to whom a sentence is addressed. Vocatives have two main functions:

- They may be used as a **call**, to gain someone's attention:

  Mike, telephone for you.
  Children, dinner-time!

- They can be used to **address** someone, expressing a particular social relationship or personal attitude:

  Doctor, I'm worried about my big toe.
  We mustn't be late, **dearest**.
  Leave it alone, **imbecile**!

- Vocatives are **optional** elements: they can be added to or removed from the sentence without the rest of the construction being affected.

- They may occur at the beginning, middle, or end of a sentence, conveying different kinds of nuance and emphasis:

  John, I'd like my aunt to sit here.
  I'd like my aunt, John, to sit here.
  I'd like my aunt to sit here, John.

Clauses

Vocatives can be:

- **Names**, with or without titles: *David, Mr Doe.*

- **Family** labels: *auntie, dad, mummy.*

- Markers of **status** or **respect**: *sir, my Lord.*

- Labels for **occupations**: *waiter, nurse.*

- **Evaluative** labels: *darling, dear, idiot, pig.*

- **General** labels: *lads, ladies and gentlemen.*

- The pronoun **you** (an extremely impolite use): *You, where's the phone in here?*

- Occasionally, certain kinds of **clause**: *Whoever you are, stop doing that.*

Some vocatives can be expanded, especially using adjectives (p.166): *old man, you fat fraud.*

Caution

A vocative belongs to a whole sentence, whatever the number of clauses. It is not an element of clause structure like subject, verb, etc.

John, **put that down** and **come over here**.
She's sure to ring back, dear, **if she has any news**.

Usage

Grammatical issues

- There is usually just one vocative per sentence, with repetition being decidedly unusual:

  Well, doctor, I've got an awful headache, and, doctor, my ear hurts, so that, doctor, I find it difficult to hear, doctor …

- A word used as a vocative does not follow the same rules of grammar as the same word used in other ways. The normal use of *handsome*, for example, allows it to be compared: *He's more handsome than Fred*. But this cannot happen as a vocative: *Come here, more handsome!*

- The vocative marker *O* is used only in religious settings (*O God, who knowest all things …*).

Social issues

In **formal** speech, and in writing, the social rules governing the use of vocatives are usually clear-cut. It is possible to consult etiquette handbooks to find out how to address people of rank in the approved way. If the rules are not followed, there may be sanctions – as in court, where participants can be cautioned for improperly addressing the judge.

In **informal** speech situations, the rules are complex and shifting. There seem always to be exceptions to even the most obvious of general statements. For example, one would expect *love* (as in *Come here, love*), to be restricted to talk between people who are on intimate terms. But it is regularly used by some bus conductors, bar staff, and others, even to people they have never met before.

- The rules governing the use of 'first names' are extremely subtle, and it is often difficult to know what usage to adopt. In recent years, they have increased in contexts where previously titles were usual (e.g. in business settings). Using a first name can also express a social attitude – such as between social worker and client, or teacher and pupil.

- The use of *sir* and *ma'am* to address strangers is much more common in American than in British English. These terms are also more formal in Britain. Often, however, people avoid using a vocative at all, gaining a stranger's attention by the use of such a formula as *Excuse me* (polite) or *hey* (impolite).

Letters (but not postcards) usually begin with a salutation in the form of a vocative, placed on a separate line before the text begins. The use of *Dear* is normal, but there are many other options.

Dear Sir

Dear Mrs Smith

Brother Joe

To whom it may concern

Gentleman!

Concord, or **agreement**, is a way of showing that two grammatical units have a certain feature in common. There are several instances of concord between clause elements.

- The most important is the 'third person' rule for verbs in the present tense (p.100). This states that singular subjects take singular verbs, and plural subjects take plural verbs.

  My cat has a meal in the evening.
  My cats have a meal in the evening.

- The verb *be* also shows first person concord between subject and verb in the present tense, using *am*. This verb is the only one to display past tense concord, with the first and third persons, using *was*.

  I am ready.   **I was** ready.   **She was** ready.

- Nouns as complements (p.64) agree with their corresponding subjects or objects in number:

  That is an **apple**.   **Those** are **apples**.
  I thought **him** a fool.   I thought **them fools**.

(For problems with pronouns, see p.165.)

Three types of concord

Grammatical concord occurs when elements formally agree with each other, as above.

Notional concord occurs when the verb agrees with the singular or plural **meaning** of the subject, regardless of any grammatical marker. In *Two **miles is** a long way*, the verb is singular because two miles is viewed as a single entity.

Concord of proximity occurs when the verb agrees with the number of a nearby noun, rather than with the real subject, as in ***No one** except his **friends agree** with him*.

Usage

People are uncertain about concord. Traditional grammars (p.32) insist on grammatical concord, but usage often favours notional concord. Concord of proximity is common in spontaneous speech, but is condemned in writing.

• Usage is particularly divided over *none*:

  None of the pens **is/are** on the table.

  The plural concord is more frequently used, but the older tradition insists on the singular.

• When two nouns are linked as subject, there is often a choice, depending on whether the meanings are seen as one or separate:

  Law and order is/are now established.

The verb element in clause structure (**V**, p.44) consists of one or more verbs comprising a **verb phrase**:

I **saw** an elephant.   I **haven't seen** one.
Did I **see** one?   I **shouldn't have been seeing** them.

These examples show that the verb phrase can consist of a single verb, known as the **main** verb, or be accompanied by one or more **auxiliary** verbs. There can be up to four auxiliaries, all going in front of the main verb.

Auxiliary verb(s)				Main verb
				kiss
			is	kissing
		has	been	kissing
	must	have	been	kissing
(rare)	must	have	been	being	kissed

> ### Caution
> A verb phrase consisting of only one verb is still known as a phrase. The main verb is seen as the nucleus, or **head**, of the potentially larger phrase.

Types of verb

Three types of verb can occur within the verb phrase.

- **Full** (or **lexical**) verbs, with a clearly stateable meaning. These act as main verbs.

  run, jump, go, look, want, think, find …

  There is no limit to the verbs in this class.

- **Modal auxiliary** verbs, which express a range of judgments about the likelihood of events. These function only as auxiliary verbs.

  will, shall, may, might, can, could …

  There are nine verbs in this class (with some marginal cases, p.88).

- **Primary** verbs can function either as main verbs or as auxiliary verbs. They are three in number: *be, have,* and *do.*

  Main verb use:
  They **are** happy.   She **has** a dog.   They **do** sums.

  Auxiliary verb use:
  They **are** going.   She **has** seen it.   **Do** they go?

Certain other verbs do not fall clearly into these three types: see p.88.

The forms of a **regular** verb can be predicted by rules. An **irregular** verb is one where some forms are unpredictable. There are thousands of regular verbs, but less than 300 irregular ones.

The forms of the regular verb

Regular full verbs appear in four forms, each of which performs a different role in the clause (p.40).

- The **base form** – a form with no endings, as listed in a dictionary (sometimes called the 'infinitive' form):

  go   run   look   discover   remember

- The **-s form**, made by adding an -s ending to the base (sometimes with a spelling change). The pronunciation of the -s varies, depending on the preceding sound.

/-s/	/-z/	/-ɪz/
looks cuts	runs tries	passes pushes

- The **-ing participle**, made by adding -ing to the base (often with a spelling change):

  visiting   begging   panicking   creating

- A form made by adding *-ed* to the base (often with a spelling change). In speech, the pronunciation of the *-ed* varies, depending on the preceding sound:

/-t/	/-d/	/-id/
passed stopped	died barred	rented funded

This ending is found in the **past form** and in the **-ed participle form**.

The past form has just one use: to express the past tense: *John kicked the ball*.

The *-ed* participle form has three uses:

- To help express a past aspect (p.104), as in

  He's kicked the ball.

- To help express the passive voice (p.96), as in

  You'll be kicked on the shin.

- To begin a clause (p.40), as in

  Kicked and bruised, he hobbled off the field.

Caution

Traditionally, *-ed* forms are 'past participles' and *-ing* forms are 'present participles', but these labels are unclear. The former is not restricted to past time (*He will be stopped*), nor the latter to the present time (*He was going*).

The forms of the irregular verb

Irregular verbs make their -s form and -ing participle by adding an ending to the base, in the same way as regular verbs. But they have either an unpredictable past tense, or an unpredictable -ed participle form, or both. Many irregular verbs therefore appear in **five** forms.

Two features of irregular verbs

- Most verbs change the vowel of the base to make their past or -ed participle forms. This process is known as vowel **gradation**.

  meet → met   take → took   speak → spoken

- The -ed ending is never used in a regular way, and is often not used at all (as in *cut, met, won*). An important pattern with some verbs is the use of a variant form, in which the /-d/ sound of the ending changes to /-t/.

  burned/burnt   spilled/spilt   kneeled/knelt

Usage

Forms such as *burned* are more common in American than in British English, but frequency varies greatly. Note that the *d* and *t* forms do not convey exactly the same nuance: the *d* form emphasises the duration of an action. Thus we tend to say *It burned for hours* but *Ow! That burnt me*.

The seven classes of irregular verb

I About 20 verbs whose only irregular feature is the ending used for both their past and *-ed* participle forms.

have/had
send/sent
burn/burnt ~ burned

II About 10 verbs whose past tense is regular, but whose *-ed* participle form has an *-n* ending, and a variant form in *-ed*.

mow/mown ~ mowed
swell/swollen ~ swelled

III About 40 verbs which have the same ending for the past and *-ed* participle forms, but this is irregular. They also change the vowel of the base form.

keep/kept
sleep/slept
teach/taught
sell/sold

IV About 75 verbs with an *-n* ending for the *-ed* participle form, and an irregular past form. The vowel of the base also changes.

blow/blew/blown
take/took/taken
see/saw/seen
undo/undid/undone

V About 40 verbs which have the same form throughout.

cut   let   shut
broadcast   outbid

VI About 70 verbs which have no ending, but use the same form for both past tense and *-ed* participle. The vowel changes from that used in the base.

spin/spun
mislead/misled
sit/sat
stand/stood

VII About 25 verbs, forming the most irregular type. There is no ending; the past and *-ed* participle forms differ; and the vowels change with each form.

swim/swam/swum
begin/began/begun
come/came/come
go/went/gone

Finite and nonfinite

Verb phrases are also classified into two broad types, based on the kind of contrast in meaning expressed by the verb: **finite** and **nonfinite**. The finite forms of the verb are those which signal contrasts of number, tense, person, and mood: the **-s form**, the **past form**, and some uses of the **base form**. The nonfinite forms do not vary in this way.

Finite verb phrases

- Show a contrast in **tense**:

  She **works** in London.   She **worked** in London.

- Show a contrast in **number** and **person** (p.160):

  He **works**.   They **work**.   I **am**.   You **are**.

- Allow the expression of facts, possibilities, wishes, and other contrasts of **mood** (p.92):

  He asked that the car **be** moved.   It **was** moved.

If there is a series of verbs in the verb phrase, the finite verb is always the first.

I **was** being kicked.   They **have** been asked.

Nonfinite verb phrases

Nonfinite forms do **not** express contrasts of tense, number, person, or mood. These forms therefore stay the same in a clause, regardless of any grammatical variation which may be taking place alongside them.

There are three nonfinite forms of the verb:

- The **-ing participle** (see also p.163)

  I'm **going**.   They're **going**.   He was **going**.
  Going home, I/we/they felt concerned.

- The **-ed participle**

  I've **asked**.   He was **asked**.   They were **asked**.
  Asked to come early, I/you/we arrived at 3.

- The **base form** used as an **infinitive**

  They might **see**.   I'll **see**.   He wants to **see**.

A clause with a finite verb phrase in it is a **finite clause**. A clause which begins with a nonfinite verb form is a **nonfinite clause**. Without an accompanying finite clause, nonfinite clauses are ambiguous:

Walking down the road.

Who is walking? How many people? When did the action happen?

Auxiliary verbs

Auxiliary (or 'helping') verbs assist the main verb in a clause to express several basic grammatical contrasts, such as in person, number, and tense (p.82). There are two kinds of auxiliary verb.

- The **primary** verbs, *be, have, do,* which can also function as main verbs (p.76).

- The **modal** verbs, which cannot be used as main verbs:

can	may	will	shall	must
could	might	would	should	

  A few 'marginal' modal verbs are described on p.88.

Primary and modal verbs do not follow the same grammatical rules. In particular:

- Primaries have **-s forms** (p.78); modals do not:

is	has	does
~~mays~~	~~wills~~	~~musts~~

- Primaries have **nonfinite forms** (p.83); modals do not:

to be	being	been
~~to may~~	~~maying~~	~~mayed~~

Some differences between auxiliary and main verbs

- Auxiliaries can be used before the word *not*; main verbs usually cannot:

  He might go. →He might not go.
  He saw me. → ~~He saw not me.~~

- The **contracted** form *-n't* can be attached to almost all auxiliaries (sometimes causing a change in their form); this is never possible with main verbs:

  can't   won't   isn't   doesn't   ~~walkn't~~

- The first auxiliary in a verb phrase is known as the **operator**. In this use, it can go before the subject in order to ask a question (p.49). This is not possible with main verbs:

  Must I go?   **Has** he been drinking?
  ~~Saw he a car?~~   ~~Asked they the way?~~

Caution

Do is known as the **empty** or **dummy** auxiliary, because it has no specific meaning (unlike *can*, etc., p.110). Its function is purely to 'stand in' as an auxiliary when the construction needs one, and other verbs would be inappropriate.

I **don't** smoke.   John **does**.   **Did** you?

Usage

There are many variations in auxiliary verb usage:

- There are alternative contracted forms:

  she isn't **vs.** she's not   I won't **vs.** I'll not

  The former type is more common in most dialects – but not in Scotland or northern England.

- *Am* is a problem. *I'm not* does not alternate with *I amn't* – though *amn't I?* can be heard in Scottish and Irish English. Standard English prefers *aren't I?* (informal) or *am I not?* (formal). *I ain't* is widely used, especially in American English, but it is not accepted as a standard form.

- *Mayn't* and *shan't* have become little used in recent years, and are almost nonexistent in American English (p.109).

- In archaic or jocular use, main verbs are sometimes used before *not*:

  I know not what to say!
  Ask not what your country can do for you; ask what you can do for your country!

The verb phrase

The *have* problem

- When *have* is used as a main verb meaning 'possess', there are two question forms:

  Have you a car?   Do you have a car?

  The former is formal, and uncommon today, especially in the past (*Had you a car?*).

- There are two answers to the *do* question:

  I have/haven't.   I do/don't.

  The latter is normal in American English, and is increasingly common in British English.

- The situation is complicated by the existence of an alternative usage with *got.* This is preferred in informal spoken British English, but it attracts criticism if used in writing.

  Have you got a car?   I've got six.

- When *have* as a main verb means 'take', etc., *do* is the normal usage:

  Do you have sugar with your tea?
  Not ~~Have you sugar with your tea?~~

- Note the difference between these uses:

  Do you have headaches? (i.e. as a rule)
  Have you got a headache? (i.e. now)

The distinction between **main verb** and **auxiliary verb** is not clear-cut. A small number of verbs occur which cannot be clearly identified as either.

- The **marginal modals** are *dare*, *need*, *ought to*, and *used to*. They are called 'marginal' because they behave in slightly different ways from the 'central' modal verbs (*will*, etc., p.84). The most important point is that they can be used either as auxiliaries:

Need we go?   Daren't she go?   Oughtn't I?

or as main verbs (allowing auxiliaries to precede them):

I shall need to go.   He doesn't dare.
You didn't ought (to). (often criticised as nonstandard)

Usage

Used to occurs only in the past tense form, and always includes *to*. We do not say ~~I use to go~~ or ~~I used go~~. In the negative form, some people prefer it as a main verb (but are often uncertain about the spelling): *I didn't use(d) to go*. Others prefer it as an auxiliary verb: *I usen't/used not to go* (especially in Britain).

- **Modal idioms** are forms like *had better, would rather, be to,* and *have got to* (often reduced to *gotta* in informal speech):

  I**'d better** go.   You**'d rather** stay?   I**'ve got to** go.
  It**'s to** take place in the morning.

  The meanings of these phrases are very like those of the modals (p.110), but their grammar is not the same. For instance, they cannot occur at the beginning of a clause:

  I may go. → I had better go.
  May I go? → ~~Had better I go?~~ (cf. Had I better go?)

  On the other hand, they are not entirely like main verbs either – for instance, they cannot follow auxiliaries: we do not say ~~I will have got to go~~.

- **Semi-auxiliaries** are forms like *be about to, be able to, be going to, be supposed to, have to,* and several others.

  I **have to** go.   You**'re able** to stay?   It's **going to** fall.

  These phrases act very like auxiliaries, but there are certain differences. Compare *I can go* → *I can't go* with *It's going to fall* → ~~It's goingn't to fall~~ (it has to be *It isn't going to fall*).

- **Catenatives** are verbs like *appear to, come to, fail to, get to, happen to,* and many more. The Latin-derived name refers to their ability to appear as a 'chain'.

  He **appeared to** see me.   He **failed to** see me.
  He **appeared to fail to want to come to** see the show.

Multi-word verbs are full verbs (p.77) which consist of more than one word. The most common type consists of a verb followed by one or two **particles**.

come in   sit down   drink up   get off
put up with   look forward to   look down on

A few multi-word verbs have a less predictable structure, and thus have to be taken as idioms:

take pride in   break even   lie low   put paid to

What can be a particle?

* Some spatial adverbs (p.178), such as *aback, ahead, aside, away, back, home, in front*.

* Some prepositions (p.188), such as *against, at, for, from, into, like, of, onto, with*.

* Some words which can act either as adverbs or prepositions, such as *by, down, in, on, over*.

Verbs taking adverb particles are known as **phrasal verbs**. Those taking prepositional particles are known as **prepositional verbs**. (Sometimes the term 'phrasal verb' is used in a general way, referring to both types.)

Phrasal and prepositional verbs do not follow the same grammatical rules. Here are two of the differences:

- Prepositional verbs need a following noun phrase (p.112); phrasal verbs can stand alone:

  The dog went for the postman.   not   ~~The dog went for.~~
  It went astray.   not   ~~It went astray the postman.~~

- When a personal pronoun (p.160) follows the verb, it occurs **before** the particle in a phrasal verb, and **after** the particle in a prepositional verb:

  They **called on** him last week.   not   ~~They called him on.~~
  They **called** him **up** last week.   not   ~~They called up him.~~

Caution

- Note the differences between such sentences as:

  I / came across / the road / on my map.
  I / came / across the road / on my bicycle.

  In the first, *come across* acts as a single unit (meaning 'find'), and is thus a multi-word verb. In the second, the two words do **not** form such a unit, but are in **free combination**: *across* goes with *the road*, and *come* has its own meaning.

- Some verbs include **both** an adverb and a preposition: the **phrasal-prepositional** verbs. These include *look forward to* and *get away with*.

Finite verb phrases (p.82) can be grouped into three broad types, based on the kind of general meaning they convey. These types, known as **moods**, show whether a clause is expressing a factual, nonfactual, or directive meaning.

- Most verb phrases are in the **indicative** mood, which is used for stating or questioning ('indicating') matters of a **factual** kind:

  It's sunny.   We aren't ready.   Is John in?

- The **subjunctive** mood is used to express wishes, conditions, and other **nonfactual** situations:

  I insisted that John **pay** on time.

  The indicative would be *I insisted that John pays on time.* It states a fact (that John **does** pay on time), whereas the subjunctive expresses a hope (that John **will** pay on time).

- The **imperative** mood is used to express **directive** utterances (p.52):

  Put it down.   Sit in the corner.

The subjunctive

The subjunctive is used very little in modern English, being mainly restricted to formal or formulaic expression. There are three patterns of use.

- The **mandative** subjunctive is found in the expression of proposals, resolutions, demands, and other 'mandatory' attitudes. It consists of the base form of the verb, and is distinctive only in the third person singular of the present tense (p.100):

  I request that he **write** to the Council.

- The **formulaic** subjunctive also consists of the base form of the verb. It is used in several fixed expressions:

  Come what may ...   Heaven forbid ...
  Suffice it to say ...   Be it noted ...

- The **were- subjunctive** (or 'past' subjunctive) expresses a hypothetical or unreal meaning, and is mainly used in clauses introduced by *if* or *though*. This form is distinctive only in the first and third person singular (p.160) of the past tense of *be*:

  If I **were** you ...   I wish it **were** finished.

Usage

- The indicative form *was* replaces *were* in informal styles: *if I was you …* . This use of *was* tends to attract criticism when it appears in written expression.

- The mandative subjunctive is much more common in American than in British English. In Britain, it is formal and somewhat legalistic in style, and tends to be replaced either by the indicative or by a construction with *should*:

I demand that he leave at once. (subjunctive use)
I demand that he leaves at once. (indicative use)
I demand that he should leave at once. (use of *should*)

The American preference seems to be currently increasing in Britain.

Caution

- Indicative sentences using modal verbs (p.84) sometimes express meanings close to imperatives and subjunctives. *You must go* is similar to *Go!*, and *she might go* to *if she were to go.*
- Some grammarians also regard the **infinitive** (p.83) as a verbal mood, on the grounds that this form also typically expresses nonfactual meaning (*To sleep, perchance to dream* …). In the present approach, however, only **finite** forms of the verb (p.82) are analysed into moods.

Suffixes that form verbs

Suffix	Add to	Example
-ate	noun	orchestrate, chlorinate
-en	adjective	deafen, quicken
-(i)fy	adjective or noun	simplify, beautify
-ize/-ise	adjective or noun	modernize, hospitalise

Usage

- The over-use of the -ise suffix attracts stylistic criticism, and new forms ending in -ise are often attacked. Forms which were criticised a generation ago (such as finalise, hospitalise and publicise) are now widely accepted. But there is still considerable opposition to more recent forms, such as privatise, prioritise, routinise, cosmeticise, coordinatise, and their associated nouns (comprehensivisation, etc.).

- The choice of -ise vs. -ize is a common cause of spelling difficulty. Some verbs are never spelled with a z (e.g. advertise, advise, arise, comprise, despise, exercise, rise). But for most verbs, -ize is the standard spelling in American English (e.g. organize, finalize, idolize, realize), and it is increasingly the form being used by British publishing houses. However, some British writers avoid -ize on principle, simply because it is American in origin!

The action expressed by the clause can be viewed in either of
two ways:

The dog saw the cat.   The cat was seen by the dog.

This kind of contrast is referred to as **voice**. The first type of
construction is known as the **active voice**. The second, which is
far less common, is the **passive voice**.

How to form passives from actives

- The subject of the active
  verb is moved to the end of
  the clause, and becomes the
  passive **agent**. *By* is added.

- The object of the active verb
  is moved to the front of the
  clause, and becomes the
  passive **subject**.

- A passive verb phrase
  replaces the active – a form
  of the auxiliary verb *be*
  (p.84) followed by the *-ed*
  participle (p.83).

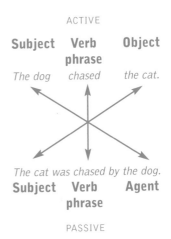

ACTIVE

Subject	Verb phrase	Object
The dog	*chased*	*the cat.*

The cat was chased by the dog.

Subject	Verb phrase	Agent

PASSIVE

Get

The passive auxiliary is usually a form of *be*. But *get* can be used to focus attention on the (usually unpleasant) event affecting the subject.

I was kicked at the match.   I got kicked at the match.

Get- passives do not usually have an agent. We are more likely to hear *I was hurt by the car* and *I got hurt,* rather than *I got hurt by the car*.

Which verbs take passives?

A **transitive** verb (p.58) can appear either as active or passive. But there are exceptions.

- Some verbs (e.g. *resemble, have, lack*) occur only in the active:

  I have a car. ➔ A car is had by me.
  Mary resembles Ellen. ➔ Ellen is resembled by Mary.

- A few verb phrases (e.g. *be said, be born*) occur only in the passive:

  She was said to be happy. ➔ Someone said her to be happy.

- If the subject and object have the same meaning, the passive is blocked:

  Mary saw herself in the mirror. ➔ Herself was seen in the mirror by Mary.

Usage

- *Get-* passives are avoided in formal style, and even in informal style are much less frequent than *be-* passives.

- Although a *by-* phrase is usually possible, it is in fact omitted in 80% of passive clauses. This is usually because the addition of an agent would be to 'state the obvious':

Jack fought Michael, and was beaten. (by Michael!)

But sometimes it is not possible to say what the agent is:

Order has been restored in the country. (by the government? the army? the police?)

And the ambiguity may be deliberate, as with this agent omission by a sheepish 10-year-old:

The cup's been smashed!

Caution

Judith was interested in grammar.

A construction of this kind is like a passive, because it has an active counterpart: *Grammar interested Judith*. But it also resembles clauses like *Judith was happy*, where *was* is followed by an adjective (p.166). Both *happy* and *interested* can be preceded by *very*, for example: *Judith was very happy/interested*. Constructions which have both verb and adjective properties are known as **semi-passives**.

The passive is infrequent in speech. In writing, it is more common in informative than in imaginative prose, especially in contexts which demand an objective, impersonal style, such as scientific publications and news reporting. The passives are highlighted in this extract from a medical textbook.

> If an air-conditioning plant **is installed**, the humidity of the nurseries **is controlled** with the heating and ventilation, but the correct humidity **can** also **be obtained** by simpler methods: for instance a humidifier or even a pan of water **can be heated** on a well-guarded gas or electric ring and the results **checked** by means of a wet and dry bulb hygrometer (Fig. 14). To ensure a humidity of 60% the wet bulb thermometer should register 65°F (18.5°C) in a nursery **kept** at 75°F (24°C), and 62°F (17°C) in a nursery **kept** at 70°F (21°C).
>
> From V. M. Crosse, *The Preterm Baby*. 7th edn. Churchill Livingstone 1971

Plain English

Never use the passive where you can use the active.

This was George Orwell's recommendation. Today, there is a strong Plain English movement in both Britain and the United States campaigning for the use of simpler, clearer, and more direct English in official forms and publications of all kinds. Both movements are opposed to the over-use of the passive. Many scientists now make less use of the passive in their writing. But passives cannot be dispensed with entirely. They give writers the option of an impersonal style, which can be very useful in contexts where it is irrelevant to state who actually carried out an action (as in the write-up of a scientific experiment):

I/John/Mary/Old Mr Smith mixed hydrogen and oxygen …
Hydrogen and oxygen were mixed …

One of the most important functions of the verb is to indicate the **time** at which an action takes place. The term **tense** is traditionally used to refer to the way the verb changes its endings to express this meaning.

Languages have different numbers of tenses, sub-dividing past, present, and future time in various ways. English has only **two** tense forms: **present** and **past**.

- The present tense uses the base form of the verb, which changes only in the third person singular, where there is an -s ending (p.78):

  I/you/we/they **go**   He/she/it **goes**

  There is also an alternative present tense form, using a form of *be*, as in *I am going* (see p.106).

- The past tense is formed by adding -*ed* to the base, in regular verbs (p.79). There are several irregular past tense forms (p.80).

  I walked   I jumped   I ran   I went

  Here too there is an alternative form using *be*, as in *I was going* (see p.106).

A future tense?

There is no future tense ending in English (unlike Latin, and some other languages). English expresses future time by a variety of other means (p.108). One of these – the use of *will* or *shall* – is often loosely referred to as the 'future tense'. But this usage changes the meaning of the word 'tense' so that it no longer refers only to the use of verb endings.

A perfect tense?

The auxiliary verb *have* (p.84) is also used to construct verb phrases, as in *I have/had walked*. Some grammarians, using Latin grammar as a model, refer to these forms as 'tenses', calling them 'perfect' and 'pluperfect' tenses. But, unlike Latin, the verb does not use a separate ending to express these meanings. For this reason, they are not described in this book as 'tenses' (p.104).

The time line

Time is often shown as a line, on which the present moment is located as a continuously moving point.

Past | Present Time | Future
Time | (includes now) | Time

But there is no identity between tense and time. Present and past tenses can be used to refer to all parts of the time line (p.102).

"I owe it all to my mother. 'Be one of those present tense writers,' she say to me when I am about twelve."

The meanings of the present tense

Three present tense uses refer to present time:
- The **state present** is used for timeless statements, or 'eternal truths':

  Oil **floats** on water.   Two and two **make** four.

- The **habitual present** is used for repeated events. There is usually an accompanying adverbial of frequency (p.178):

  I go to town **each week**.   He **drinks a lot**.

- The **instantaneous present** is used when the action begins and ends approximately at the moment of speech. It is very commonly used in demonstrations and sports commentaries:

  Smith **passes** the ball … He **shoots** …

Three present tense uses refer to other times:
- The **historic present** describes the past as if it were happening now:

  I **hear** you've resigned.

- In jokes and imaginative writing, a similar use promotes **dramatic immediacy**:

  We **look** outside (dear reader) and we **see** an old man …

- With some time adverbials (p.178), the present tense helps to refer to a specific course of action in **future** time:

  We **leave** tonight.

The meanings of the past tense

Most uses of the past tense refer to an action or state which has taken place in the past, at a definite time, with a gap between its completion and the present moment. Specific events, states, and habitual actions can all be expressed using the past tense:

I **arrived** yesterday. (event)   They **were** upset. (state)
They **went** to work regularly. (habitual)

The past tense used for the present or future

- The **attitudinal past** reflects the speaker's tentative state of mind, giving a more polite effect than would be obtained by using the present tense:

  Did you want to go? (cf. **Do** you want to go?)

- The **hypothetical past** expresses what is contrary to the speaker's beliefs. It is especially used in *if-* clauses (p.179):

  If you **worked** hard ... (you don't)
  I wish I **had** a bike. (I haven't got one)

- In **indirect speech** (p.218), a past tense used in the verb of 'saying' allows the verb in the subordinate clause to be past tense as well, even though it refers to present time:

  Did you say you **had** no money? (now)

Verb aspects

Aspect refers to how the time of action of the verb is regarded – such as whether it is complete, in progress, or showing duration. There are two types of aspectual contrast: the **perfective** and the **progressive**.

Perfective aspect

The perfective aspect is constructed by using the auxiliary verb *have* (p.84). It occurs in two forms.

* The **present perfective** is primarily used for an action continuing up to the present. This meaning of 'current relevance' contrasts with the past tense meaning (p.103):

  I**'ve lived** in Bonn for a year. (I still do)
  I **lived** in Bonn for a year. (I no longer do)

  Have you **been** to the show? (it's still on)
  Did you **go** to the show? (when it was on)

* The **past perfective** also expresses 'anterior time', but referring to the past tense:

  I **was** sorry that I **had** missed seeing John.
  (cf. I **am** sorry that I **have** not seen John.)

Specific events, states, and habitual actions can all be expressed using the perfective aspect.

He **has/had** built a car. (event)
The house **has/had** been empty for years. (state)
He**'s/'d** done it often. (habitual)

Usage

- In American English, there is a tendency to use the past tense instead of the present perfective:

American	British
Did you eat?	Have you eaten?
Did you ever see 'Lear'?	Have you ever seen 'Lear'?
You told me already.	You've told me already.
Did they come home yet?	Have they come home yet?

- Different kinds of adverbials (p.175) are associated with the past tense and the present perfective.

I saw John yesterday / a week ago / on Tuesday.
I've not seen John since Monday / so far / up to now.

Using the wrong adverbial is a common English learning error:

~~I've seen him a week ago.~~
~~I didn't see you since Monday.~~

He asked
– 'Have you eaten?'

Progressive aspect

Be can be used along with the -*ing* form of the main verb (p.78) to express an event in progress at a given time. This is the **progressive** (or **continuous**) aspect. It is used with both tenses and with both perfective aspects (pp.100, 104). Nonprogressive forms are known as **simple** forms.

Simple	Progressive
They run	They're running
They ran	They were running
They've run	They've been running
They'd run	They'd been running

With the progressive, the usual implication is that the activity is taking place over a limited period, and is not necessarily complete. By contrast, the simple aspect tends to stress the unity or completeness of the activity. Compare:

I read a book yesterday. (all of it)
I was reading a book yesterday. (it's unfinished)

Specific **events**, **states**, and **habitual actions** can all be expressed using the progressive.

Event: He blows his whistle. (a brief blast)
He's blowing his whistle. (continuous or repeated)

State: We live in France. (permanently)
We're living in France. (at present)

Habitual: He writes his own programs. (regularly)
He's writing his own programs. (as a temporary measure)

Stative vs. dynamic

Verb meanings can be grouped into **stative** and **dynamic** kinds. With dynamic meanings, the agent is actively involved in a specific action (e.g. *kick, speak, put*). Stative meanings identify processes or states of being in which no obvious action takes place (e.g. *be, have, hear, know*).

Statives do not usually occur in the progressive:

I was happy.	~~I was being happy.~~
I have a car.	~~I'm having a car.~~
I see a car.	~~I'm seeing a car.~~

But in special contexts, the progressive use is possible, giving the verb a 'dynamic' sense:

Who **am** I **seeing** in clinic this morning?

There are some interesting contrasts in meaning:

The neighbours are friendly. (routine)
The neighbours are being friendly. (why?)

Usage

- Less than 5% of all verb phrases appear in the progressive form. They are most frequent in conversation.

- The **perfective progressive** (e.g. *have been asking*) is felt to be very awkward when used in the passive voice (p.96):

  These questions **have been being** asked for months.

English has no future tense ending (p.101), but it has several
ways of expressing future time.

- **Will/shall/'ll** followed by the infinitive (*I'll see* you then)
  or the progressive (*I'll be seeing* you, implying 'as a
  matter of course'). This is by far the commonest use.

- **Be going to** followed by the infinitive: *I'm going to* ask
  him. This common informal use suggests the event will
  take place very soon.

- The **present progressive** (p.106), stressing the way a
  future event follows on from an arranged plan: *The match
  is starting* at 2. The happening is usually imminent.

- The **simple present** (p.100), often implying definiteness:
  I leave soon.   *Go before I do.*

- The use of **be to** (= future plan), **be about to** (= near
  future), and other **semi-auxiliaries** (p.89):
  She's to sit here.   *She's about to go.*

- Other **modals** (p.84) also have future meaning, e.g.
  I may/might travel by bus.

Usage

Some traditional grammars insist on a sharp distinction between the use of *will* and *shall*.

- To express **future time**, they recommend the use of *shall* with first persons (p.160) and *will* with second and third persons: *I/we shall go, You/he/she/it/they will go.*

- To express an **intention to act** ('volition', p.110), they recommend *will* with the first person and *shall* with the others: *I/we will go, You/he/she/it/they shall go.*

On this basis, sentences such as *I will be 20 soon* are condemned as wrong, because, it is said, we cannot 'intend' to be a certain age. However, modern spoken usage does not observe the *will/shall* distinction, and it has largely disappeared in several varieties (notably, American, Scottish, and Irish English). It is now rare to find *shall* in the second and third person (*Shall you go?, Mary shall sit there*), except in the most formal of styles, and it is becoming less common in the first person (p.86). *Will* is today the dominant form.

Modern usage variation prominently displayed

The function of the modal verbs (*will, may*, etc., p.84) is to reflect our judgment about whether what we say or write is true. They express a wide range of meanings:

- **Permission**, **obligation**, and **volition** (our intention to act) – meanings which are all to do with our ability to control events.

- **Possibility**, **necessity**, and **prediction** – meanings to do with our judgment about what is likely to happen, the events being outside our control.

The main meanings of the modals

can	possibility ability permission	Everyone can make mistakes. Can you remember? Can we go now?
may	possibility permission	You may be right. You may use my pen.
must	necessity obligation	There must be some mistake. We must wear our uniforms.
will	prediction volition	Oil will float on water. We won't stay long.
shall	prediction volition (p.109)	Shall I win the election? What shall we do this evening?

- Children are usually taught *may* as a more polite alternative to *can*. '*Can I get my book, Miss?* ' may, in an attempt to instil awareness of the difference, receive an ironic teacher response, '*You can, but you **may** not.*'

But on second thoughts, Kevin, you can...

Caution

Traditional grammars sometimes class the modals into pairs, calling one 'present' and the other 'past': *can/could, will/would,* s*hall/should,* and *may/might.* However, this distinction operates clearly only in indirect speech (p.218), when there is a change from present to past:

It **may** rain.   He **said** it **might** rain.

In other contexts, the *could* series has little to do with past time, expressing such meanings as tentativeness, politeness, possibility, and permission. Compare *Can you be here at 3?* with the more tentative *Could you be here at 3?.*

Might we come in?
Could/might I see your licence?
Would you hold this a moment?
Why should they object?

The noun phrase is the main construction which can appear as the subject, object, or complement of a clause (pp.60–66). It consists essentially of a **noun** or noun-like word which acts as the centre, or **head**, of the phrase. Sometimes the noun appears on its own; more often, it is accompanied by one or more other constituents (which are often described as **qualifying** the noun).

Head

Buns taste nice.
The buns taste nice.
All the buns taste nice.
All the currant buns taste nice.
All the currant buns in the window taste nice.

Noun phrases appear in all shapes and sizes. They are much more varied in their construction than the verb phrase (p.76). This extract from a newspaper article shows some of the variety that exists. The noun phrases are highlighted in bold.

United equalised on the stroke of half-time. The tireless Jones was at the front of a fine three-man move which left space for Ferguson to score from close range.

After the break, the game went in all directions until the teams settled down ten minutes into the second half. There was one moment of excitement when ...

The constituents of the noun phrase

No matter how complex a noun phrase is, it can be analysed into one or more of these four constituents:

- The **head**. This is the obligatory item, around which any other constituents cluster. The head controls the concord (p.74) with other parts of the sentence: *The **car is** outside / The **cars are** outside.*

- The **determiner**, which appears before the noun. This constituent decides what kind of noun is in the phrase – such as definite, indefinite, proper or common. Words such as *a, all* and *many* are determiners (p.136).

- The **premodification**, which comprises any other words appearing before the noun, apart from the determiners – mainly adjectives or adjective-like words, such as *red, interesting, happy* (p.144).

- The **postmodification**, which comprises all items appearing after the head. The possibilities here are described on p.146.

Some noun phrases

Determiner	Premodification	Head	Postmodification
		Fred	
my		car	
the	tall	tree	
all the	currant	buns	in the shop
some	new	books	that I shall need

Caution

- The word **phrase** normally refers to a **group** of words which work together as a clause element. But quite often a phrase may consist of only one word – in the case of noun phrases, the head noun. It may seem odd to talk about a noun phrase consisting of just one single noun. The reason is that this noun always has **potential** to be expanded into a larger phrase.

I like **books**.
I like **those books**.
I like **those red books on the table**.

- There are several kinds of 'noun-like' words which can function as the head of a noun phrase. The chief category is the **pronoun** (p.154):

The three cats	are eating	**the meat**.
They	are eating	**it**.

Note that the traditional label **pronoun** is somewhat misleading. A 'pronoun' does not refer only to a noun, but to a whole noun phrase. In the above example, *they* replaces more than just the word *cats*: we do not say *The three they*!

A few kinds of **adjective** (p.166) can also function as the head of a noun phrase.

The **Chinese** are more numerous than the **Welsh**.
The **good**, the **bad**, and the **ugly**.

Finding the head

There is often more than one noun in a noun phrase. How can we decide which is the head?

The **boy with the books** seems hungry.

One test is to see which noun controls the verb. In this case, it must be *boy*:

The **boys** with the books **seem** hungry.
The **boy** with the books **seems** hungry.

Also, we can see which noun phrase is essential to complete the meaning of the clause. *Boy* fits, whereas *book* does not:

The boy seems hungry.   ~~The book seems hungry~~.

Simple and complex noun phrases

The determiner and noun together make up the **simple noun phrase**. If other constituents are present, we have a **complex noun phrase**.

This distinction is based on the fact that there are a fixed number of determiners, and these are used to express a very small range of meanings (such as quantity, p.137). By contrast, the number of items which can appear as the other constituents is theoretically unlimited – as is suggested by this advertising caption.

Why do you think we make Nuttall's Mintoes such a devilishly smooth cool creamy minty chewy round slow velvety fresh clean solid buttery taste?

The traditional definition of a **noun** says that it is the name of a person, place, or thing. But this definition is extremely vague, and it does not tell the whole story.

- The vagueness is in the word 'thing'. *Advice, beauty,* and *consequence* are nouns, but it is difficult to see what 'things' these words refer to.

- The definition makes no reference at all to the way nouns actually behave in the grammar of the language.

How grammar identifies words as nouns

A word is a noun if some of these factors apply:

- Its meaning and use is decided by one of the determiners, e.g. *a, the, some* (p.136).

- It acts as the head of the noun phrase (p.112).

- It changes its form to express singular and plural (p.122), or the genitive case (p.132).

- It uses a special ending (**suffixes**, p.232) which is attached to verbs (**V**), adjectives (**Adj**), or other nouns (**N**), e.g. *boy* →*boyhood.*

Suffixes that form nouns

Abstract nouns			**Concrete nouns**		
Suffix	**Add to**	**Example**	**Suffix**	**Add to**	**Example**
-age	N	*mileage*	-ant	V	*contestant*
-age	V	*wastage*	-ee	V	*referee*
-al	V	*refusal*	-eer	N	*profiteer*
-ation	V	*exploitation*	-er	N	*villager*
-dom	N	*kingdom*	-er	V	writer
-(e)ry	N	*slavery*	-ese	N or Adj	*Chinese*
-ful	N	*spoonful*	-ess	N	*waitress*
-hood	N	*boyhood*	-ette	N	*kitchenette*
-ing	N	*carpeting*	-(i)an	N or Adj	*Parisian*
-ing	V	*building*	-ist	N or Adj	*loyalist*
-ism	N	*idealism*	-ite	N or Adj	*socialite*
-ity	Adj	*rapidity*	-let	N	*booklet*
-ment	V	*amazement*	-ling	N	*duckling*
-ness	Adj	*kindness*	-or	V	*survivor*
-ocracy	N	*democracy*	-ster	N	*gangster*
-ship	N	*friendship*			

Noun classes

Nouns can be grouped into six main classes. The first division is into **proper** and **common** nouns. Common nouns can then be divided into **count** and **noncount** types. And both of these can be further divided into **concrete** and **abstract** types. Each class is described on pp.118–120.

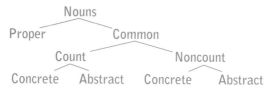

Proper nouns are names of specific people, places, times, occasions, events, publications, and so on. They differ from **common nouns** in three main ways.

- Proper nouns can stand alone (*Fred is here, I like London, Today is Tuesday*), whereas only certain common nouns can (*Book is red, Egg is bad, I like cat, Chess is fun*), see p.120.

- Proper nouns do not usually allow a plural (*Londons, Freds, Everests*), whereas most common nouns do (*books, eggs, pens, musics*), see p.122.

- Proper nouns are not usually used with determiners (*a London, the Fred, some France*), whereas common nouns are (*a book, the music, some bread*), see p.136.

When proper nouns of time refer to specific periods, or to more than one occasion, they behave very like common nouns: *I hate Mondays, We left on the Sunday.*

I am Fred, a <u>proper</u> noun but you are the king, a <u>common</u> noun.

- Proper nouns are written with an initial capital letter. But not all words with initial capitals are proper nouns (e.g. the ironic *That's a Big Deal!*). Also, there is sometimes uncertainty in writing as to whether a word should be considered proper or common: *the bible* or *the Bible*? *the moon* or *the Moon?*

- There is a big difference between *the Oxford road* (= one of several roads which lead to Oxford) and *the Oxford Road* (= the name of a specific road leading to Oxford). When the name of a road becomes completely established within a community, the article drops: *Oxford Road*.

Caution

- A proper noun is a single word. But many **proper names** consist of more than one word: *John Smith, Park Lane, King's College*. In these cases, the nouns work together as a single unit.

- Names like *The Hague* look as if they are being used with the definite article, but *The* is part of the name in such cases. It cannot be omitted, changed, or separated: we cannot say ~~Hague, A Hague,~~ or ~~The beautiful Hague~~.

- In special contexts, proper nouns can behave like common nouns: *Look at **all those Smiths!**, I used to know **a John Brown**, They've changed **my London**.*

30

Count and noncount nouns

Common nouns (p.118) can be divided into two types. **Count nouns** refer to individual, countable entities, such as books, eggs, and horses. **Noncount nouns** refer to an undifferentiated mass or notion, such as butter, music, and advice. Noncount nouns are also known as **mass** nouns.

---

* Count nouns cannot stand alone in the singular (*Book is red*); noncount nouns can (*Chess is fun*).

* Count nouns allow a plural (*books, eggs*); noncount nouns don't (*musics*).

* Count nouns occur in the singular with *a* (*a book*); noncount nouns with *some* (*some music*). Both types can occur with *the* (*the book/music*).

Abstract and concrete nouns

Both count and noncount nouns can be divided further into **abstract** and **concrete** types. Concrete nouns refer to entities which can be observed and measured (*book, car, butter*, etc.). Abstract nouns refer to unobservable notions (*difficulty, music, remark*, etc.).

Many noncount nouns have an equivalent countable expression
using such words as *piece* or *bit* (**partitive nouns**) followed by
of:

information	a piece of information
luck	a piece of luck
applause	a round of applause
grass	a blade of grass
bread	a loaf of bread

Caution

Some nouns can be either count or noncount, depending on
their meaning. *Cake*, for example, is a count noun in this
sentence:

Would you like a cake?

But a noncount noun in this one:

Do you like cake?

There are many such pairs:

The lights and sounds were amazing. (count)
Light travels faster than sound. (noncount)

I like those lambs. (count)
I like lamb. (noncount)

31 Variable nouns: singular and plural

Most nouns have both a **singular** and a **plural** form, showing a contrast between 'one' and 'more than one', and these are known as **variable** nouns. A small group of cases do **not** have a number contrast – the **invariable** nouns (p.126).

Most variable nouns change from singular to plural in a wholly predictable way, by adding an *s* ending. This is the **regular** plural form, as seen in *dogs, flutes, eggs, pterodactyls, dictionaries*, and thousands more. By contrast, there are only a few hundred nouns with an **irregular** plural form. Ironically, it is this minority which attracts the grammarian's interest, as these are the ones which lead to difficulties in language learning.

* Seven nouns change their vowel:
  man → *men, foot* → *feet, goose* → *geese, mouse* → *mice, woman* → *women, tooth* → *teeth, louse* → *lice.*

* Three nouns add *-en* – in two cases changing the vowel sound as well:
  ox → *oxen, child* → *children, brother* → *brethren* (in religious contexts only).

* A few nouns change their final /-f/ to /-v/ and add /-z/ such as:
  knife → *knives, wife* → *wives, leaf* → *leaves, half* → *halves.*

The noun phrase

Nouns of foreign origin

Nouns which have been borrowed from foreign languages pose a particular problem. Some have adopted the regular plural ending: *Let's sing three more choruses* (not ~~chori~~). Some have kept the original foreign plural: *More crises to deal with!* (not ~~crisises~~). And some permit both: *What lovely cactuses/cacti!* There are no rules: people have to learn which form to use as they meet the words for the first time.

Some foreign plurals from Latin and Greek

-**us** words *circus* → *circuses*
But *stimulus* → *stimuli*   *bacillus* → *bacilli*
    focus → *focuses/foci*

-**a** words *area* → *areas*
But *alga* → *algae*   *larva* → *larvae*
    formula → *formulas/formulae*

-**um** words *museum* → *museums*
But *addendum* → *addenda*   *erratum* → *errata*
    aquarium → *aquariums/aquaria*

-**ex/ix** words *codex* → *codices*
But *index* → *indexes/indices*
    appendix → *appendixes/appendices*

-**is** words *metropolis* → *metropolises*
But *basis* → *bases*   *crisis* → *crises*

-**on** words *electron* → *electrons*
But *criterion* → *criteria*   *automaton* → *automata*

31

Several nouns have the same form for both singular and plural. If you hear someone say *I like your sheep*, there is no way of knowing, just from the language, whether the focus of their affection is a single animal or a group. These nouns do not add an ending when they are used in the plural, so they have come to be called **zero plurals**.

Like *sheep* are the names of some other animals (such as *deer* and *cod*) and nationalities (*Japanese*, *Swiss*), several nouns expressing quantity (*quid*, *p* = 'pence', *ton*), and a few others (such as *aircraft, offspring, innings, crossroads, kennels*).

Compound nouns

Compound nouns combine two or more words into a single unit. They usually form the plural by adding *s* to the last element, as in *babysitters* or *gin-and-tonics*. In a few cases, it is the first element which takes the ending: this happens especially when a particle (p.90) is included, as in *passers-by* and *men-of-war*. And sometimes there is a choice:

spoonsful	courts martial	mothers-in-law
spoonfuls	court martials	mother-in-laws

The irregular ending is the more formal usage. Very rarely, both elements change their form – as when *woman doctor* becomes *women doctors*.

The noun phrase

A few irregular nouns have two plurals – such as *hoofs* and *hooves*, *scarfs* and *scarves*. Some people insist on distinct pronunciations in such cases – and distinct spellings. But there is nowadays a noticeable tendency to replace all these irregular forms by the regular ending *s*.

Caution

• In most cases, the distinction between singular and plural corresponds to that between 'one' and 'more than one'. But look out for the exceptions. For example, *foliage* is singular, and *leaves* is plural, yet both refer to a multiplicity of objects. Similarly, *wheat* and *oats* refer to the same number of things, but one is singular and the other plural.

• Regular plurals are formed, it is said, by 'adding an *s*'. But it is not quite so simple. This 's' has several sounds and spellings.

In **speech**, the /s / ending of *cats* differs from the /z/ of *dogs* and the /ɪz / of *horses*.

In **writing**, there are several rules: some words add *-es* (*boxes*); some add *-es* and also change a letter (*skies*); some double a letter (*quizzes*); and some add an apostrophe before the *s* (*1960's*). A few words even have **two** spellings, such as *cargo(e)s*, *banjo(e)s*, and *volcano(e)s*.

Many nouns do not show a contrast between singular or plural: the **invariable** nouns. These are usually classified into two types: those used only in the singular, and those used only in the plural.

Used only as singular nouns

- *John, London,* and other proper names (p.118):

  John was at the party.
  Not ~~Johns were at the party~~.

- *physics, mumps, billiards,* and several other names of subjects, diseases, and games:

  Physics is fun.
  Not ~~Physics are fun.~~

- *music, homework, beer, snow,* and many other nouns when used in a noncount way (p.120):

  Music is the food of love.
  Not ~~Musics are the food of love~~.

  Where the noun is used in a countable way, of course, a plural is possible: compare *Beer is best* and *I'll have three beers.*

Used only as plural nouns

- *scissors, binoculars, jeans,* and other names of 'two-part' items (and where, to form the singular, we have to say 'a pair of'):

  Your jeans are on the table.
  Not Your jeans is on the table.

- *amends, annals, banns, congratulations, dregs, outskirts, remains, stairs, thanks,* and several other nouns ending in -*s*:

  The outskirts are pretty uninspiring.
  Not The outskirts is pretty uninspiring.

- *people, folk, police, cattle, poultry, livestock,* and several other nouns which have a 'zero' ending (p.124):

  The police are outside.
  Not The police is outside.

Two plurals

Several animal names have two plurals – regular and 'zero': *shrimp, rabbit, fish, duck,* etc. But there is a subtle difference in meaning. Are we thinking of the animals as individuals or as a category of game? The professional hunter *goes shootin' duck* – never *ducks*. And passers-by at the local pond take their children to *feed the ducks* – never *feed the duck* (unless, of course, the pond contains only one)! Usage varies over *fish* vs. *fishes*.

Usage

- With a small group of nouns, usually ending in *s*, people sometimes argue over whether they should be used as singulars or plurals. Is it *The headquarters is three miles away* or *The headquarters are three miles away*? In most cases, the answer is 'it depends'. The two meanings slightly differ. The singular suggests the idea of a single entity, whereas the plural emphasises that the entity is made up of individual units. Like *headquarters* are *barracks, aircraft, steelworks*, and a few others.

- The noun *data* causes special problems. This word was once found only as a plural, but it is now often used as a singular, especially in scientific contexts: *Much of this data needs re-examining* (rather than *Many of these data need re-examining*). This use continues to attract critical comments from those who prefer the older pattern. As a result, professionals often feel sensitive about the word, and some even try to avoid using it.

- New singular usages have also appeared with the words *media* (in the sense of 'mass media'), *criteria*, and *phenomena*: *The media is responsible, The criteria is important, The phenomena was amazing*. Criticism of singular *media* seems to be reducing, as its use becomes increasingly widespread, but educated people universally condemn the singular use of the other two words.

Caution

- Some nouns may **look** plural, but they are not used as plurals:

    Here **is** the news.
    Mathematic**s** **is** my worst subject.
    Billiard**s** **is** becoming very popular.

    And some can be both singular and plural, depending on their meaning:

    Politics **is** a complex subject.
    Fred's politics **are** boring.
    Darts **is** easy.   Your darts **are** broken.

- Some nouns may **look** singular, but they are not used as singulars:

    The police are standing by. (Singular: *a police officer, policeman*, etc.)
    The cattle were grazing peacefully.
    Those vermin need to be exterminated.

Other such nouns are *livestock, poultry, folk* (as in *country folk*), and *people*. *People* is particularly interesting, as it acts as the normal plural of *person* (*one person ~ many people*); but both of these nouns can additionally be used with regular plurals.

Several persons were seen entering the premises. (legal)
The English-speaking peoples of the world.

In many languages (such as Latin or French), nouns can be grouped into types, based on the kind of endings they have, or on the way they pattern with other words in the noun phrase (p.112). For example, in French, nouns preceded by *le* ('the') form one type, known as **masculine**. Those preceded by *la* ('the') form another, known as **feminine**. This is a classification of grammatical **gender**.

English does not make use of grammatical gender. But it does have ways of distinguishing **animate** beings from **inanimate** entities, **personal** from **nonpersonal** beings, and **male** from **female** sexes. We simply observe which nouns and pronouns go together (*he, she, it, who, which*, etc., see p.154).

Here is a box. **It** is the box **which** was …
Here is a man. **He** is the man **who** was …

Caution

Grammatical **gender** should not be confused with the natural **sex** of a person or animal. 'Males' are not always 'masculine', as far as grammar is concerned; nor are 'females' always feminine. In German, for example, the word for 'girl' (*das Mädchen*) is neuter!

- **Inanimate** nouns (*box, advice*) pattern only with *it* and *which*. **Animate** nouns make varying use of *he/she* and *who*, and are divided into personal and nonpersonal types.

- **Personal** animate nouns refer to males and females, and pattern with *he/she/who*: e.g.*boy/girl, host/hostess*. Some nouns can be either 'he' or 'she' (they have **dual gender**), such as *artist, cook, cousin, singer* (p.165).

- **Nonpersonal** animate nouns refer to animals. Most take *it/which*, but those with a special place in human society take *he/she/who*, and some even have distinct male/female forms: *bull/cow, dog/bitch, tiger/tigress*. The 'lower animals' (ants, cod, etc.) do not normally take *he/she*.

Collective nouns (*committee, team, army, family*, etc.) can take either *it/which* or *they/who*.

The committee which has met ... It ...
The committee who have met ... They ...

The difference is one of point of view: the singular stresses the impersonal unity of the group; the plural the personal individuality of its members.

Usage

Some nouns vary, depending on whether they are thought of in an intimate way. Vehicles and countries often take *she* (*France has increased her exports*). Pets are often *he/she*, and a bawling baby may even be *it*!

34 Case

In many languages, nouns have endings which show how the noun phrase is being used within the clause – such as whether it is acting as a subject or object (p.44). The set of endings is known as the case system. English does not have a complex case system, like the one which was used in Latin. There are only two cases: a **common** case, where the noun has no ending at all, and the **genitive**.

The genitive is made by adding an *s* to the singular form of the noun. In writing, this appears with a preceding apostrophe: *the girl's books*. With most plural nouns, an *s* ending is already present (p.122), so the written form adds a following apostrophe (*the girls' books*). In a few irregular cases, *'s* is used (*the men's books*). In speech, there is no difference in sound between *girls* and *girls'*.

Not all singular nouns add an ending. There are a few exceptions where the only signal is the apostrophe:

- Greek names of more than one syllable, ending in *-s*: *Socrates' work*, not ~~*Socrates's work*~~.

- Some fixed expressions: *for goodness' sake*.

Names ending in /-z/ vary in usage: we find both *Dickens's novels* and *Dickens' novels*.

The meanings of the genitive

The chief meaning of the genitive case is **possession**: *my son's bike = his bike*. But the case is used to express several other meanings too.

* To express an **origin**: *the girl's story*.

* To **describe** something: *a summer's day*.

* To **measure** a period: *ten days' leave*.

* To express the role of **subject**: *the boy's application* (that is, *the boy applied*).

* To express the role of **object**: *the boy's release* (that is, *someone released the boy*).

The *of-* genitive

There is a close similarity between a noun in the genitive case and the same noun preceded by *of* (the ***of-* genitive**):

the ship's name ~ the name of the ship

The choice is largely based on factors of gender and style. Personal nouns and the higher animals (p.131) tend to take the genitive ending; inanimate nouns take the *of-* genitive. Compare *Fred's book* with ~~the book of Fred~~, and ~~the problem's part~~ with *a part of the problem.* The genitive is also used with geographical names (*China's future*) and with many nouns of special relevance to human activity (*my life's aim, the body's needs*).

34

Special uses of the genitive

There are four special uses of the genitive case:

- The **group genitive** occurs when the genitive ending is attached to a noun which **follows** the head noun of the phrase:

  the **teacher's** book   but   the teacher of **music's** book

  The possessor is the teacher, not the music; but the ending nonetheless is added to *music*.

- The **independent genitive** occurs when the noun following the genitive is omitted, because the context makes it obvious:

  Mary's bike is newer than **John's**.

- A similar use is found when the genitive refers to premises or establishments: the **local genitive**:

  We ate at **Bert's**.
  I'm going to the **dentist's**.
  We visited **St Paul's**.

- It is sometimes possible to have both the genitive ending and the *of-* construction simultaneously: the **post-genitive**:

  some friends **of my uncle's**   an invention **of Smith's**

  This usage expresses a less definite meaning than the alternative: *my uncle's friends, Smith's invention.*

The apostrophe was introduced into English in the sixteenth century, and became widespread during the seventeenth. But there was much uncertainty about its use, especially in the plural, even until the middle of the nineteenth century. Then grammarians laid down rules saying how it should be used (p.132).

During the twentieth century, uncertainty re-emerged. There is now a strong tendency to omit the apostrophe. This is not entirely due to a lack of education. Many modern signwriters and typographical designers, for example, think that the apostrophe is fussy and old-fashioned.

Around the turn of the twentieth century, the apostrophe came to be dropped from the name of many banks and large businesses (e.g. *Lloyds, Harrods*). Today it is almost always omitted in shop signs, placards, and other notices. On the London Underground, the signs say *St Pauls* and *Earls Court*. In Oxford Street shops, we find *Ladies wear* and *Mans shop*.

As a result of these changing attitudes, many people nowadays feel unsure about the correct use of the apostrophe, and add it before plural endings and verb endings: *We sell fresh pie's, Everyone like's our chips.* This usage is universally condemned by educated writers.

Homemade shepherds pie's

HUDSONS PIE SHOP

35

Determiners

Noun phrases express a range of meanings, some of which are more definite and specific than others. These meanings are conveyed through a small set of words which precede the noun, such as *a*, *the*, *some*, and *those*. Words of this kind, which 'determine' the number and definiteness of the noun phrase, are known as **determiners**.

There are three kinds of determiner: **central determiners**, **predeterminers** (p.140), and **postdeterminers** (p.142).

Central determiners

The central determiners consist of the **definite article** (*the*), the **indefinite article** (*a*(*n*)), and a few other words which can take their place, such as *this*, *that*, *each*, *every*, *some* and *any*. These words **never** co–occur with an article:

a cat   each cat   this cat   some cats
a~~ this cat~~   ~~the my cat~~   ~~some the cat~~

Words like *this* and *some* are called determiners only when they precede a noun. If they occur alone, standing in for a noun, they are then being used as **pronouns** (p.154):

I have some food.   I have some.
     DETERMINER   PRONOUN

           The noun phrase

Types of central determiner

	Occurs with singular count noun?	Occurs with plural count noun?	Occurs with noncount noun?(p.120)
Type 1	**yes**	**yes**	**yes**
the	*the cup*	*the cups*	*the fun*
my, etc.	*my cup*	*my cups*	*my fun*
no	*no cup*	*no cups*	*no fun*
what, etc. (p.157)	*what cup*	*what cups*	*what fun*
Type 2	**no**	**yes**	**yes**
no determiner	*cup*	*cups*	*fun*
some/any	*some cup*	*some cups*	*some fun*
enough	*enough cup*	*enough cups*	*enough fun*
Type 3	**yes**	**no**	**yes**
this, that	*that cup*	*that cups*	*that fun*
Type 4	**no**	**yes**	**no**
these, those	*these cup*	*these cups*	*these fun*
Type 5	**yes**	**no**	**no**
a(n)	*a cup*	*a cups*	*a fun*
each, every	*each cup*	*each cups*	*each fun*
(n)either	*either cup*	*either cups*	*either fun*

Caution

There are always a few exceptions. For example, *some* meaning 'a particular' is used with a singular count noun (*That's some car!*, *It's just some dog barking*). *Every* is occasionally used with a possessive word: *my every action*. Count nouns drop the determiner when used as a vocative (p.70): *Sit down, child.*

The article system comprises three concepts: the **definite article** (*the*), the **indefinite article** (*a*(*n*)), and the absence of an article (the **zero article**). Their use affects the meaning of the noun phrase – in particular, allowing us to think of nouns in a **specific** way, referring to individuals (*A/the cat is eating*) or in a **generic** way, referring to a general class or species (*A/the cat is an interesting animal, Cats are nice*).

The definite article

- *The* can refer to the immediate situation or to someone's general knowledge: *Have you fed the cat?*, *In the Great War* ...
- *The* can refer back to another noun (**anaphoric reference**): *She bought a car and a bike, but she used the bike more often.*
- *The* can refer forward to the words following the head noun (**cataphoric reference**): *I've always liked the wines of Germany.*
- *The* can refer to human institutions that we sporadically use, attend, observe, etc: *I went to the theatre, I watched the news.*

The indefinite article

- *A*(*n*) does not assume that a noun has been mentioned already. In *The book arrived*, the speaker assumes we know which book is being referred to; in *A book arrived*, there is no such assumption.

- *A*(*n*) often expresses a general state of affairs, or a notion of quantity: *I'm training to be a linguist, a hundred, six times a day*.

The zero article

The article is often omitted in idiomatic usage when talking of human institutions and routines, means of transport, periods of time, meals, and illnesses: *go to bed, travel by car, at dawn, in winter, have lunch, got flu*.

Usage

- The use of *a* or *an* varies before a few words beginning with *h*, such as *hotel* and *historical*. The latter form is often felt to be old-fashioned, though it has begun to re-emerge in recent years.

- *The* is pronounced /ði:/ (as in *thee*) in emphatic speech. Some people object to the widespread use of this form by radio and television reporters.

Words which can be used before the central determiners in the noun phrase (p.112) are known as **predeterminers**. These can be grouped into a very few types, nearly all of which express notions of quantity.

- *all*, *both*, *half*:

  all the people   both the cats   half the gold

- *double*, *three times*, etc. (**multipliers**):

  double your money   twice the cost

- *a quarter*, *one-third*, etc. (**fractions**):

  one-third the time   a quarter the amount

- *such*, *what* (used in exclamations, p.54):

  Such a fuss!   What a nice day!

It is not usually possible to use two predeterminers in the same noun phrase:

both all the people   such twice occasions

But note *all such issues*.

Caution

- Other words sometimes appear before the determiner, restricting the meaning of the noun phrase. These **restrictive** words include such adverbs as *just*, *only*, and *especially* (p.182).

  Only the two books were left.
  It's **just** a cat.

  These are not predeterminers, because they are used with the same meaning before other kinds of word:

  He's just finished.   She's only tired.

- *All*, *both*, and *half* can be used without a following noun. They then have to be analysed as **pronouns** (p.154):

  Give me half.   Both arrived.

- Some predeterminers can be followed by *of* – in which case they are also analysed as pronouns: *all of the people*, *half of it*. The *of* can be left out when the following word is a noun (*all the people*); but it is obligatory when the following word is a pronoun (*half it*).

- *All* and *both* as pronouns can also be used after the head noun – and even later in the clause, after the first auxiliary verb (p.84):

  All the people were asked.
  The people all were asked.
  The people were all asked.

38

Postdeterminers

Words in the noun phrase which follow central determiners (p.136), but precede adjectives (p.166), are known as **postdeterminers**. There are four main types.

• *one, two, three*, etc. (**cardinal numerals**):

  my **three** fat cats   the **fifty** sheep

• *first, second, last, next*, etc. (**ordinals**):

  the **first** explosion   the **last** big party

• *much, many, (a) few, (a) little, several* (a very limited set of **quantifiers**):

  the **many** people   your **several** pets

• a set of informal quantifiers consisting of a noun plus *of*: *lot of, number of, bags of*, etc.:

  a **lot of** books   a **great deal of** interest

Ordinals and cardinals may co-occur, usually in that order: *the first three times*. When the order alters, the meaning usually changes. Compare: *the **last two** pages of this book* and *the **two last** pages of these books*.

The noun phrase

Few, little, many, and *much* have comparative and superlative forms (p.172):

few/fewer/fewest houses
little/less/least money

many/more/most houses
much/more/most money

There is a popular tendency to use *less* and *least* with count nouns (p.120), but this usage is often criticised:

I've got less cards than you. (for *fewer cards*)
He's made the least mistakes. (for *fewest mistakes*)

- Especially in American English, there is a tendency to replace *number* by *amount* with count nouns: *There was a large amount of people in the hall.* This usage is also widely criticised.

Caution

- Note that *a few* and *a little* act as single units, even though they are two words. This is shown by their use with plurals (*a few books*, where ~~a books~~ is not possible) and noncount nouns (*a little music*, where ~~a music~~ is not possible).

- We need to distinguish *a little* as a quantifier, meaning 'not much', from *a + little*, meaning 'small'. In some contexts, there may be ambiguity: *I'll have a little cake, please.*

39

Premodification

Any words appearing between the postdeterminer and the head of the noun phrase (p.113) are said to **premodify** the noun (some grammars say **qualify** the noun). Premodifiers mainly consist of adjectives, but two other categories also commonly occur.

- **Adjectives** (p.166): *a **lovely** day*   *a **small round** table*

- **Participles** (p.79): *a **crumbling** wall*   *a **stolen** car*

- **Nouns** (p.116): *those **country** roads*   *a **tourist** spot*

There are also some less common types of premodification, such as the use of phrases and clauses:

We have a **round-the-clock** service here.
She's asked **I don't know how many** people.

Caution

A premodifying adjective can **itself** be **premodified** by intensifying words (p.174):

That's a **very** good point.
She's an **extremely** nice girl.

The noun phrase

Order of premodifiers

Premodifying words can appear in long sequences, but there are restrictions on their order. Compare:

a nice big cardboard box   ~~a cardboard big nice box~~

Four main zones are involved, as shown in this example:

I've got the same big red garden chairs as you have.
            I   II III   IV

I Adjectives with an absolute or intensifying meaning come first, in the **precentral** zone: *same, certain, entire, sheer,* etc.

II Other adjectives come next, in the **central** zone: *big, slow, angry, helpful,* etc.

III Participles and colour adjectives come in the **postcentral** zone: *missing, deserted, stolen, red, green,* etc.

IV Nouns, and words closely related to nouns, come in the **prehead** zone: *American, tourist* (*board*), *medical, social,* etc.

Words **within** each category may also co-occur (*American medical practice, stolen red car*), and here too there are restrictions of order. We do not normally say ~~red stolen car~~. Words which refer to inherent or visually observable properties of the noun tend to be placed next to it.

Any words appearing after the head noun within the noun phrase (p.113) are said to **postmodify** the noun.

There are three main kinds of postmodification:

- There may be **prepositional phrases** (p.188):

  the car **in the garage**   the boy **by the tree**

- There may be **nonfinite clauses** (p.83):

  the car **parked in the street**
  the man **running away**
  the film **to see**

- There may be **finite clauses** (p.83):

  the car **which was parked in the street**
  the man **who was running away**
  the film **that I saw**

There are also two minor types of postmodifier:

- using **adverbs** (p.174):

  the journey **back**   the way **out**   ten **o'clock**

- using **adjectives** (p.166):

  something **different**   the president **elect**

- Often, **more than one** construction is used as part of the postmodification:

  the car / with a red roof / parked outside / which you liked / …

  But sequences of this kind can become unwieldy, and they must be used carefully to avoid ambiguity. Compare:

  The man in the corner looking at the picture
  (the man is in the corner)

  The man looking at the picture in the corner
  (the picture could be in the corner)

  The ambiguity in the second sentence arises because it is not clear whether *in the corner* relates to *man* or *picture*.

- Sometimes a sentence is not strictly ambiguous, but it permits a bizarre interpretation – such as the idea of hats walking in *the man in a hat walking down the street*. Constructions of this kind attract criticism. A related problem arises with 'dangling participles': *Hunting for fleas on her mate, the teacher watched the gorilla*.

- Similarly, although long postmodifying sequences may not break any grammatical rules, they quickly become difficult to understand, and are generally avoided:

  I saw the car that was parked in the street near the cinema where we saw the film that you went to in the coat which you borrowed from Mary.

The most complex kind of postmodification in the noun phrase is a finite clause (p.83) introduced by the set of pronouns *who(m), whose, which, that,* or 'zero'. These are the **relative pronouns** (p.157), and the clause they introduce is known as the **relative clause**.

I can see the girl **who was waiting**.
I can see the man **to whom I spoke**.
I can see the boy **whose bike was stolen**.
I can see the books **which are on the shelf**.
I can see the egg **that you wanted**.
I can see the egg **you wanted**.

As these examples show, there is concord (p.74) between the relative pronoun and the head noun (called the **antecedent**). *Who(m)* or *whose* are used when the noun is personal; *which* is used when it is nonpersonal. *That* and zero can be used with both types: *the boy (that) I spoke to, the table (that) I bought.*

There may also be number concord between the head noun and the verb in the relative clause:

The **man** who **was** angry has calmed down.
The **men** who **were** angry have calmed down.

Some relative clauses refer back to whole sentences, not just to nouns: *He likes grammar – which is remarkable.* These are known as **sentential relative clauses**.

Relative pronouns as clause elements

In many sentences, the relative pronouns carry out the role of a clause element (p.44). We can see this if we 'interpret' the relative clause:

The boy **who saw the cat** has gone home.
Who saw the cat? **The boy** saw the cat.

Here, *who* and *the boy* are **subjects** of their clauses.

In the following sentence, however, the relative pronoun acts as an **object** element:

The car **that I bought** has gone wrong.
What did I buy? I bought **the car**.

And in the next sentence, it acts as an **adverbial**:

She left the day **on which I was ill**.
When was I ill? I was ill **on that day**.

Usage

When the personal relative pronoun *who* acts as the object in the clause, there is divided usage. In formal speech and writing, *whom* is preferred. In informal contexts, people use *who* or zero (which is in fact more common):

That is the man whom I saw. (formal)
That's the man (who) I saw. (informal)
That is the man to whom I spoke. (formal, p.195)
That's the man (who) I spoke to. (informal)

Restrictive and nonrestrictive

There are two ways in which a relative clause relates to the head noun, as can be seen from these two sentences:

My brother who's abroad has sent me a letter.
(my other brothers haven't)

My brother – who's abroad – has sent me a letter.
(he is the only brother I have)

In the first case, the relative clause is needed in order to identify what the noun is referring to; it 'restricts' the noun to mean 'the brother I am talking about'. This is therefore known as the **restrictive relative clause**.

There is no such restriction in the second sentence: the relative clause provides optional, extra information which could be omitted without affecting the noun's identity – 'My brother has sent me a letter'. This is known as the **nonrestrictive relative clause**.

Some grammars use different terms, and talk about **defining** and **nondefining** clauses.

In writing, the two types of clause are distinguished by punctuation marks. The nonrestrictive clause is usually preceded and followed by a comma or (as above) a dash. In speech, the contrast can be made by adding pauses on either side of the nonrestrictive clause, or by altering the intonation (p.242), so that the head noun is said in a more prominent manner.

Choosing the right kind of relative clause can be critical. Compare these sentences:

Snakes which are poisonous should be avoided.

Snakes, which are poisonous, should be avoided.

The use of the restrictive clause (the first sentence) implies that only **some** snakes are poisonous, which is true. But the use of the nonrestrictive clause implies that **all** snakes are poisonous, which is false.

Quite correct – Only some snakes are poisonous.

Caution

Relative clauses need to be distinguished from a second type of finite clause which can postmodify a noun: the **appositive** clause (p.152). This looks very similar to a relative clause introduced by *that*. Compare:

The story that I wrote was published.
The story that I had resigned was published.

The first is relative (*that* can be replaced by *which*); the second is appositive (*that* means 'that is', and cannot be replaced by *which*).

We sometimes find two or more noun phrases acting together as a single element of clause structure. There are two ways in which this can be done:

- By **coordination** (p.204), where there is no identity of meaning between the noun phrases:

  I saw **an elephant and a tiger**.
  I'd like **a beer, crisps, and some cheese**.
  He's got **no money, no job**.
  I need **a car or a bike or a train**.

- By **apposition**, where the two noun phrases do have the same meaning:

  I saw **my brother, the town clerk**.
  Mr Smith, my neighbour, called to see me.
  He sent **his reply, namely, a letter**.

There is a clear difference between coordination and apposition, as can be seen from these sentences:

John and the butcher came to see me.
(Two people came: coordination.)

John, the butcher, came to see me.
(One person came: apposition.)

Types of apposition

There are several kinds of meaning expressed by the relationship of apposition, such as the following.

- The two noun phrases are **equivalent** in meaning, with one providing the name or specific identity of the other:

  I spoke to **my neighbour, Mr Smith**.

- One noun phrase provides a **rewording** of the other:

  He's **a philologist – that is, a linguist**.

- One noun phrase expresses an **attribute** of the other:

  I saw **the clerk, a rather seedy type**.

- One noun phrase **includes** the other:

  I like **big films, for example *Gandhi***.

- It is also possible to analyse some **proper names** (p. 119) as examples of apposition. In these cases, the identity of one noun depends on the presence of the other (as in restrictive relative clauses, p.150). Thus, *Mount Fuji* can be glossed as 'the Mount which is Fuji'. And a similar analysis can be made of *Farmer Jones, Quebec Province, President Bush, Queen Elizabeth, Mississippi River, Oxford Street*, etc.

Pronouns are words which stand for a noun, a whole noun phrase (p.112), or several noun phrases, or which refer directly to some aspect of the situation. In each case, the meaning expressed is much less specific than that found in phrases containing nouns.

- Replacing a **noun**:

  I've got a red car and Mike's got a brown **one**.

- Replacing a **noun phrase**:

  My cousin Nell's arrived. **She**'s had a long journey.

- Referring to a very general concept which includes the meaning of **many noun phrases**:

  Is **anyone** there? (where *anyone* includes boys, girls, men, women, etc.)

  I can see **something** in the distance.

- Referring to some unspecified aspect of the **situation** surrounding the speaker or writer:

  Look at **that**! (pointing)
  He's going to crash.
  It's going to be a lovely day.

Characteristics of pronouns

- Pronouns carry out a similar range of functions to **noun phrases**. For example, they can appear as subject, object, or complement of the clause (p.44):

  She saw **me**.   **That**'s **him**.   Give **it** to **them**.

- Pronouns are different from nouns in that they do not usually permit **modification**:

  a big car   a big it
  a man outside   a he outside

- Some pronouns have different **cases** (p.132) for subject and object functions, whereas nouns do not:

  I vs. me   who vs. whom   he vs. him

- Some pronouns show a contrast between personal and nonpersonal **gender** and between male and female (p.164):

  he/she vs. it   who vs. which

- Several pronouns distinguish singular and plural **number**, but not simply by adding an *s* (p.122):

  I vs. we   he vs. they

- Some pronouns have different **persons** (p.160):

  I vs. you vs. he, etc.

There are many words which can act as a pronoun, but they express different kinds of meaning, and they do not all follow the same grammatical rules.

- The **central** pronouns express contrasts of person, gender, and number (p.164). They all express a **definite**, specific meaning. There are three types:

  - **Personal pronouns** are the main means of identifying speakers, addressees, and others (p.160): *I, you, he, she, it, we, they.*

  - **Reflexive pronouns**, always ending in *-self* or *-selves*, 'reflect' the meaning of a noun or pronoun elsewhere in the clause: *myself, yourself,* etc.

    John shaved **himself**. They washed **themselves**.

  - **Possessive pronouns** express ownership, and appear in two forms.
    My, your, his, etc. are used as determiners in the noun phrase (p.136):

    my car   **her** bike.

    Mine, yours, his, hers, ours, etc. are used on their own:

    This is **mine**. **Hers** is on the table.

- **Reciprocal pronouns** are used to express a 'two-way' relationship: *each other, one another.*

  They blamed **each other.**

- **Relative pronouns** are used to link a relative clause (p.148) to the head of the noun phrase: *who, whom, whose, which* and *that.*

- **Interrogative pronouns** are used to ask questions about personal and nonpersonal nouns: *who, whom, whose, which, what.* They permit a contrast between definite and indefinite meaning:

  What did you buy? (indefinite: an open choice)
  Which did you buy? (definite: you chose from a small number of alternatives)

- **Demonstrative pronouns** express a contrast between 'near' and 'distant': *this/these, that/those.*

  Take **this** here, not **that** over there.

Usage

This/that have other uses. With nouns of time, *this* refers to 'what is to come', *that* to 'what has been' (*this week* vs. *that week*). *This* may be used to introduce a new topic in familiar speech (*I saw this girl …*). *That* may express dislike (*She's awful, that Mabel!*).

- **Indefinite pronouns** express a less specific meaning than the pronouns listed on pp.156–7. This meaning is always to do with **quantity**. There are two main types:

- **Compound pronouns** consist of two elements:

  every-   some-   any-   no- + -one   -body   -thing

  Someone must have seen something.

- ***Of*- pronouns** consist of several forms which may appear alone, or be followed by *of*. They express a range of meanings, from the 'universal' sense of words like *all* and *each* to the 'negative' sense of words like *none* and *few*.

  all, both, each, much, many, more, most,
  a few/fewer/fewest, a little/less/least,
  some, any, one, none, neither, few, little

  He's eaten **all of** the cake.   I have **none**.
  Few spoke.   **Neither of** them went.

Usage

- All compound pronouns except *no one* are written as single words: *everything, nobody*, etc.

- Pronouns ending in *-one* are more frequent, and are usually considered more elegant, than those ending in *-body*.

Caution

- *Each* and *every* can be used as determiners (p.136), but only *each* can be used alone as a pronoun: *each of them*, ~~*every of them*~~. *Every* must be followed by *one*: *every one of them*. Note that *every one* differs from *everyone*: the former can refer to things (*every one of the cakes*), whereas the latter refers only to people.

- *Each, both, one, either, neither, many, few* and *a few* refer to count nouns; *much, little* and *a little* to noncount nouns (p.120). The remaining pronouns can refer to either.

  many cakes ~~many music~~
  ~~a little cakes~~ a little music
  some cakes some music

- *One* has three uses. It has a numerical sense (*Have one of these*). It can substitute for a singular or plural noun (*Is this the one you want?*, *Are these the ones?*). And it can be used with the meaning 'people in general' (*One would think not*). This last use can be very formal: *One should see one's doctor, shouldn't one?*

- *Some* carries a positive implication; *any* a negative one. *Did someone phone?* suggests that the speaker was expecting a call. *Did anyone phone?* makes no such suggestion. Hence the greater politeness of *Would you like some cake?* over *Would you like any cake?* The latter hints that the addressee might not wish to accept.

The **personal pronouns** occur more frequently, and have more special characteristics than any other type of pronoun. They are called 'personal' because they refer to the people involved in the act of communication.

- The **first person** includes the speaker(s) or writer(s) of the message:

  I, me, my, mine, myself
  we, us, our(s), ourselves

- The **second person** includes the addressee(s), but excludes the speaker(s) or writer(s):

  you, your(s), yourself, yourselves

- The **third person** refers to 'third parties', i.e. excluding the speaker(s), writer(s) or addressee(s):

  he, him, his, himself, she, her(s), herself
  it, its, itself; one, one's, oneself
  they, them, their(s), themselves

It is part of the personal pronoun system, even though it refers to nonpersonal entities.

My, *your*, *one's* and *their* are used only as determiners (p. 137), and never as independent forms.

- *We* has several special uses. Although it is the 'plural' pronoun, it can refer to a single person: the 'royal' or 'editorial' *we*, where it replaces *I*: *We are not amused*. It can also refer to the addressee, especially when talking 'down' to someone: *How are we today?* (said by a doctor to a patient). And it can refer to a third party, as when one secretary might say to another about their boss, *We're in a bad mood today*.

- *You* and *they* can refer to people in general, or to some group within society: *You can't get a good pint nowadays, They keep putting fares up*.

- *Thou/thee/thy/thyself/thine* are found in religious use, but with considerable variation. The current trend is to replace them by *you-* forms. They are also occasionally heard in some rural northern British dialects.

- There are several nonstandard pronoun forms, notably for the second person. *Youse* is common in northern US English, Irish English, and in parts of Britain (such as Liverpool and Glasgow). In Southern US English, a new plural form has developed: *you-all* (or *y'all*).

- *It* can be used with very little meaning, to refer in a general way to time, distance, atmospheric conditions, or life in general.

What time is it?   It's lovely out.   How's it going?
Isn't it a shame?   I take it you're going.

The pronoun is here called **empty** or **prop** *it* (p.225).

Personal pronouns have a genitive form, as have nouns (p.132); but they also have an **objective** form, which nouns do not have. This form is primarily used when the pronoun is the object of the clause, and also after a preposition. When the pronoun is subject of the clause, it appears in the **subjective** form.

I/we/he/she/they saw me/us/him/her/them
    SUBJECTIVE   OBJECTIVE

Who has also got an objective form, *whom* (p.149), and a genitive form, *whose*.

Caution

The genitive forms of the personal pronouns – *my/mine, our(s), your(s), his, her(s), its* and *theirs* – are traditionally described under a separate heading: the **possessive** pronouns (p.156).

- In certain contexts, the objective form is used where grammatical tradition recommends the subjective:

Who's there? It's **me**. (for *It is* ***I***.)
He's as tall as **her**. (for *He is as tall as* ***she***.)
Ted and **me** went by bus. (for *Ted and* ***I*** *went by bus.*)

These usages attract varying degrees of criticism in a formal setting. *Me* as a single-word reply is now used by almost everyone, and attracts little comment. The *X and me* construction, however, is often criticised, especially when speakers reverse the normal order of politeness, and put the *me* first: *Me and Ted went by bus.*

As a result of the long-standing criticism of *me*, there is now a widespread sensitivity about its use, and this has led people to avoid it, even in parts of the clause where its use would be grammatically correct:

Between you and I ... (for *you and me*)
He asked Mike and I to do it. (for *Mike and me*)

- There is also uncertainty over the correct form in sentences such as *It's no use my/me asking him*. Older grammars analyse words like *asking* as 'verbal nouns', or **gerunds**, and insist on the use of the possessive pronoun (or the *'s* form of a noun: ... *John's asking him*). Modern grammars do not usually use the term gerund: *asking* would be analysed as a verb (the *-ing* participle, p.83) – as can be seen from the way it takes an object, *him*. The possessive is the preferred usage in a formal style, especially if the item is a pronoun or a short, personal noun phrase. The alternative is more common informally.

A contrast of male and female **gender**, based mainly on the sex of a person or animal (p.132), is restricted to two of the third person singular pronouns:

he/she   him/her   his/her(s)   himself/herself

The various forms of *I*, *you*, *it*, *we*, and *they* are sex-neutral.

Sexual bias

Since the 1960s, the movement towards sexual equality in society has directed attention to the male bias present in language, in such forms as *chairman* and the *man in the street*. With pronouns, the chief criticism has been directed at the use of the masculine third person pronoun to refer 'generically' to people in general, or to a group comprising both sexes.

A new student will find **he** has a great deal to do.
The applicant should sign **his** name at the bottom.
A writer should ask **himself** three questions ...

Criticism of this usage has led to the search for other forms of expression, but there is no simple alternative, and people who wish to avoid a male bias often have to rethink the structure of a sentence.

Ways of avoiding male pronoun bias

- Change the construction to a **plural**:

  New students will find **they** have a lot to do.

  However, this solution causes problems when the indefinite pronouns (*everyone*, *anybody*, etc., p.158) are used:

  Everyone knows **they** should attend the show.
  Someone's been objecting, haven't **they**?

  Here the singular forms are made to agree with a plural pronoun *they*, which goes against the general practice of standard English. This construction therefore tends to be restricted to informal use.

- Use **both** third person pronouns. This usage is generally felt to be awkward:

  Each applicant has to sign **his or her** name.

- Invent a **new** sex-neutral pronoun:

  S/he can apply for a grant.

  This form is useful, but it exists only in writing. In speech, there have been more radical suggestions, especially in America, for a new pronoun. Many new forms have been proposed (e.g. *hesh*, *po*, *man*, *hir*, *co*), but none has yet attracted widespread support.

Words which express some feature or quality of a noun or pronoun are traditionally known as **adjectives**. To decide if a word is an adjective, several criteria are available.

- An adjective can premodify a noun (p.144): *a big book*, *the tall man*. This is known as the adjective's **attributive** function.

- An adjective can occur alone as a complement (p.64): *The book is big*, *He is tall*. This is the adjective's **predicative** function.

- An adjective can be premodified by *very* and other **intensifying** words (p.174): *very big, terribly tall*.

- An adjective can appear as a **comparative** or a **superlative** (p.172). Some adjectives use *-er* and *-est* endings to express these contrasts: *taller, tallest*. Others use *more* and *most*: *more beautiful, most beautiful*.

- Many adjectives permit the addition of *-ly* to form an **adverb** (p.175): *sad → sadly, great → greatly*. There are several exceptions, however: ~~*oldly, tallly*~~.

Adjective suffixes

Many adjectives have no distinctive ending (*big, fat,* etc.), but there are a few suffixes which typically signal that a word is an adjective.

Suffix	Add to	Result	Suffix	Add to	Result
-able	verb	*washable*	*-less*	noun	*restless*
-al	noun	*musical*	*-like*	noun	*childlike*
-ed	noun	*ragged*	*-ly*	noun	*friendly*
-esque	noun	*romanesque*	*-ous*	noun	*desirous*
-ful	noun	*hopeful*	*-some*	noun	*bothersome*
-ic	noun	*heroic*	*-worthy*	noun	*praiseworthy*
-ish	noun	*foolish*	*-y*	noun	*sandy*
-ive	verb	*effective*			

Central and peripheral

To count as an adjective, a word must be able to function in both attributive and predicative positions. The vast majority of adjectives are like this (e.g. *big, red, tall, infinite*), and these are known as **central** adjectives. Words which can appear in only one or other of these positions are **peripheral** adjectives (e.g. *asleep, utter*). Further examples are on p.169.

a big table	the table is big
an infinite universe	the universe is infinite

~~the asleep dog~~	the dog is asleep
utter nonsense	~~the nonsense is utter~~ (p.169)

There may be other differences within each class: compare *very big* and *~~very infinite~~*, *~~bigly~~* and *infinitely*.

The functions of the adjective

Adjectives can appear in other parts of the clause apart from attributive and predicative positions (*the happy dog / the dog is happy*, p.166).

- They can appear as **complement** to the object (p.64):

  He made her **happy**.   I pushed the door **open**.

- They can appear after the noun (be **postpositive**) in a few fixed phrases, and after compound pronouns (p.158):

  heir apparent   time immemorial   me included
  B sharp   proof positive   anything useful

- Certain adjectives which refer to well-known groups of people can appear as the **head** of a noun phrase (p.112):

  the innocent   the French   into the unknown

- They can act as a shortened (**verbless**) clause:

  I saw his face, dirty and scratched.
  (i.e. which was dirty and scratched)

  Come tomorrow, if possible.
  (i.e. if this is possible)

- They can be used as an **exclamation**: *Marvellous!*

Peripheral adjectives

- Some adjectives are found only in **attributive** position:

an outright lie	~~the lie is outright~~
utter folly	~~the folly is utter~~
his chief excuse	~~his excuse is chief~~
my former friend	~~my friend is former~~
a criminal court	~~a court is criminal~~

- Some adjectives are found only in **predicative** position:

The girl felt unwell.	~~the unwell girl~~
The man was loath to leave.	~~the loath man~~

Caution

- Adjectives can be modified by other words. They are then the head of an **adjective phrase**:

That's **very nice**.
That house is **larger than mine**.
I'll find someone **clever enough to go**.

- Some adjectives have more than one use. In *a poor man*, *poor* is a central adjective, because it can appear in both positions (*The man is poor*). *Poor* is opposed to *rich*. But in the phrase *Oh, you poor man!* (said to someone who has fallen over), *poor* is peripheral. It has an idiomatic meaning which does not allow the use of *The man is poor*. *Poor* is not opposed to *rich*.

There are many words which display some properties of the adjective and some properties of another word class. They can be grouped into three types.

- **Adjective or adverb?** Some words can be used either as an adjective or as an adverb (p.174):

Adjective	Adverb
It was **late** afternoon.	They arrived **late**.
It's a **fine** view.	It looks **fine**.
I got an **early** train.	We finished **early**.

- **Adjective or noun?** Nouns can be used before the head of the phrase, and thus appear to be adjectives (p.144). But they do not act like adjectives in any other way:

  the town clock   ~~the clock is town~~   ~~the towner clock~~

- **Adjective or participle?** Some adjectives have the same endings as verb participles in *-ing* or *-ed* (p.79), e.g. *interesting, deserted*. Where there is no corresponding verb, the word must be an adjective: *his talented wife* (there is no verb *to talent*). But in other cases, we need to see whether the word acts as adjective or verb:

  She is (very) calculating. (adjective)
  She is calculating our salaries. (participle)

Words beginning with *a*

There are several words beginning with
a- which present grammarians with a
problem. Some grammars call them
adjectives; others call them adverbs.
They are words like:

aboard ablaze abroad
ajar   alike alone
afraid around away
adrift aloof aware

Some of these words function more like adjectives; others are
more like adverbs:

• All these words can be used after *be*, but if the word is really
  adjective-like, it can be used after other **copular** verbs (p.64)
  as well, such as *seem*:

  The child seemed asleep/alert/alone/awake.
  ~~The child seemed abroad/around/away/aboard.~~

• Conversely, if the word is adverb-like, it can be used after
  verbs of **motion**, such as *go*:

  We went abroad/around/away/aboard.
  ~~We went afraid/alone/awake/alert.~~

Most of these words, it seems, are more like adjectives than
adverbs. But not all of them take *very*, and only a few of them
can appear attributively: *very alone*, but ~~*very afire*~~; *an aloof
manner*, but ~~*an ajar door*~~, ~~*an ablaze barn*~~. They are plainly a
very exceptional group.

Adjective comparison

Most adjectives can be compared in one of three ways. The quality they express can be related to a **higher** degree, to the **same** degree, or to a **lower** degree.

• Comparison to a higher degree is shown by adding -*er*/-*est* (the **inflectional** form), or by using *more*/*most* (the **periphrastic** form):

Mary is **taller**. Jean is the **tallest**.
This is **more** interesting than that.
This is the **most** interesting book I've seen.

• Comparison to the same degree is shown by the use of *as* (sometimes *so*) ... *as*:

This is **as** big **as** that. This is not **so** big.

• Comparison to a lower degree is shown by the use of *less*/*least*:

This is **less** heavy. That's the **least** heavy.

The base form of the adjective is the **absolute** form. The construction with -*er*/*more* is the **comparative** form, and that with -*est*/*most* is the **superlative** form.

The choice between *-er/-est* and *more/most* is largely based on how **long** the adjective is.

- Adjectives of **one syllable** usually take *–er/-est*, though the *more/most* forms are sometimes used: *thin/thinner/thinnest*. *Real, right*, and *wrong* occur only with *more/most*: *That's a more real situation* (not *~~realler~~*).

- Adjectives of **two syllables** appear in both forms: *That's a quieter/more quiet spot.* Those ending in *-y, -ow, -le, -er,* and *-ure* favour the inflection: *happy, narrow, gentle, clever, obscure*, etc. *Proper* and *eager* are exceptions: they use only *more/most*.

- Adjectives of **three syllables** or longer use *more/most*: *more/most beautiful* (*~~beautifuller/beautifullest~~*). These forms are also used when participles (p.79) occur as adjectives: *a worn suit ~ more/most worn* (not *~~worner/wornest~~*). Adjectives beginning with *un-* are exceptions, as they also permit endings: *unhappier/unhappiest*.

Caution

Good/better/best and *bad/worse/worst* are irregular. *Far* has two forms: *further/farther* and *furthest/farthest*. The *-a-* forms are less common, being mainly used to express physical distance (as in the *farthest north*). *Old* has regular forms (*older/oldest*) and also an irregular use (*elder/eldest*) when talking about family members.

The **adverb** is the most heterogeneous of all the word classes in English grammar. It contains words which perform a wide variety of functions within the sentence.

Adverbs have two main functions:

- They can be an **adverbial** clause element, performing different kinds of role within the clause (p.180):

  We're travelling **tomorrow**.
  Frankly I'm not interested.

- They can **premodify** a word or phrase, most often an adjective or another adverb (p.144):

  You sounded **terribly** anxious. (+ adjective)
  You spoke **very** anxiously. (+ adverb)
  I spoke to **nearly** everyone. (+ pronoun, p.154)
  We had **quite** a party. (+ noun phrase, p.112)

In addition, certain adverbs have other functions. Some adverbs (especially of time and place) can **postmodify** a word or phrase (p.146): *the day **before**, my trip **abroad**, someone **else***. Some can also follow a **preposition** (p.188): *Come over **here**!, He should have done it by **now***.

Types of adverb

- **Simple** (one-element) adverbs, such as *just, only, soon*.

- **Compound** adverbs, such as *somehow, therefore, whereby*.

- Adverbs ending with a **suffix** (p.232), usually *-ly* added to an
  adjective: *quickly, sadly, fortunately*. A few other suffixes are
  also found, especially in informal speech:

cowgirl-**fashion**   new-**style**   earth**wards**
side**ways**   clock**wise**

Coinages such as *physics-wise* are particularly common
in American English, but many people find this type of
construction objectionable, and prefer an alternative
phrasing (such as *in terms of physics*).

Caution

An adverb is a **single** word. However, there are many cases
where a **multi-word** construction performs the same
function. For example, adverbs often act as the head of a
phrase (an **adverb phrase**, such as *very **happily** indeed*). A
whole clause (p.40) may function as an adverb (an
adverbial clause, such as *They left **when their car was
fixed***). And **prepositional phrases** (p.188) are amongst
the commonest kinds of adverbial (*They went **in the car***).

Adverbial is the general term which is used for **all** these
types of construction (p.68).

The adverbial is the most 'mobile' element in the clause (p.68). We can see this by taking a clause and testing whether a particular adverbial can be used at different places in its structure. With some clauses, the adverbial can appear at up to seven places.

The adverb *originally* can be inserted at any of the points marked ⋏ in the following sentence:

⋏ The book ⋏ must ⋏ have ⋏ been ⋏ bought ⋏ in the shop ⋏.

On the other hand, there are restrictions governing the position of many adverbials:

She **soon** went home.   ~~She went **soon** home.~~
I travelled **by bus**.   ~~I **by bus** travelled.~~

And the position of the adverbial can alter the meaning of the clause:

He smiled at her **happily**. (gave a happy smile)
Happily, he smiled at her. (it was fortunate that he smiled at her)

Usage

Many people have strong stylistic objections to the use of an adverbial between *to* and the infinitive form of the verb. This is the **split infinitive** construction.

You ought to **seriously** consider the problem.

I want you to **regularly** attend these meetings.

Objections to this construction have been voiced for well over a century, on the grounds that the 'unity' of the infinitive should not be broken; today many educated people are extremely sensitive about the usage. Some try consciously to avoid it, especially in writing, and strongly criticise it when they hear it used.

The construction is however frequently heard in informal speech, especially in such sentences as:

I told him to **jolly well** try again.
We would like to **so** organise the system that we all keep busy.
I'm going to **really** get down to work.

And often it is difficult to see what alternative there is to splitting the infinitive. Re-positioning can produce an unidiomatic or awkward construction:

We would like so to organise the system ...
We would like to organise so the system ...

The adverbial element conveys a wide range of meanings.

- **Space** adverbials, including the notions of **position**, **direction** ('to' and 'from'), and **distance**. They usually answer the question 'where?'.

  They live **in a bungalow**. (position)
  She walked **to the school**. (direction to)
  It came **from here**. (direction from)
  We drove **for fifty miles**. (distance)

- **Time** adverbials, including the notions of **position**, **duration**, **frequency**, and the **relationship** between one time and another. They usually answer the question 'when?'.

  I arrived **on Sunday**. (position)
  I stayed **for a week**. (duration)
  We go there **often**. (frequency)
  I've been there **already**. (relationship)

- **Process** adverbials, including the notions of **manner**, **means**, **instrument**, and **agent** (p.96). They usually answer the question 'how?'.

  I ate **slowly**. (manner)
  I spoke **with notes**. (means)
  I ate **with my fork**. (instrument)
  I was stung **by a bee**. (agent)

- **Respect** adverbials, expressing the notion of 'being concerned with'. They answer the question 'with respect to what?'.

  I can't see the difficulty **over John**.
  She's advising me **on legal matters**.

- **Contingency** adverbials, including such notions as **cause**, **reason**, **purpose**, **result**, **condition** and **concession**. Many of these adverbials relate to the questions 'why?' or 'with what result?'.

  She died **of pneumonia**. (cause)
  I went **because I had the money**. (reason)
  I went **in order to find out for myself**. (purpose)
  I worked hard, **so I passed the exam**. (result)
  You'll see him **if you run**. (condition)
  Although he was tired, he decided to stay up to see the New Year in. (concession)

- **Modality** adverbials, including such notions as **emphasis**, **approximation**, and **restriction**:

  I **certainly** agree with you. (emphasis)
  They've **hardly** seen anything. (approximation)
  I was **only** asking. (restriction)

- **Degree** adverbials, including such notions as **amplification**, **diminution**, and **measure**:

  I **badly** want a drink. (amplification)
  I did help her **a bit**. (diminution)
  I'm quite satisfied that you've answered my questions **sufficiently**. (measure)

Adverbials (p.68) function in a clause in four different ways: as **adjuncts**, **subjuncts**, **disjuncts**, and **conjuncts**. Each class has a different range of meanings and follows different rules. The largest class comprises the **adjuncts**.

Adjuncts are adverbials which relate directly to the meaning of the verb (**modify** the verb, some grammars say), or to the whole sentence:

loudly, tomorrow, afterwards, accidentally, quickly, along the road, next week, often, when the car stopped, because it was broken, in order to arrive on time

Sentence and predication adjuncts

Certain adjuncts seem to modify the whole sentence, rather than just the part centring on the verb (the **predication**). They are therefore known as **sentence adjuncts**. They can occur both at the beginning of a clause and at the end.

The dog bit her **on Friday**.
On Friday the dog bit her.

Predication adjuncts occur naturally only at the end.

The dog bit her **on the leg**.
~~On the leg the dog bit her.~~

The adjunct is the only type of adverbial that behaves like the other clause elements, such as subject and object (p.44). Several of the grammatical rules which affect them affect adjuncts too. The remaining three types behave in very different ways, and are not so closely involved in clause structure (see pp.182–7).

Two important similarities between adjuncts and other clause elements:

- They can be the **focus** of a sentence (p.223): *John saw Jim outside*, for example, can vary in several ways.

  It was **John** who saw Jim outside. (focus on the subject)
  It was **Jim** who John saw outside. (focus on the object)
  It was **outside** that John saw Jim. (focus on the adjunct)

- They can be the answer to a **question**:

  Who saw Jim? John.
  Where did John see Jim? Outside.

Caution

Not all possible sequences of adjuncts are acceptable. Shorter items tend to appear before longer ones, and the following order is common: **respect** + **process** + **space** + **time** + **contingency**. *We spoke quietly in the bar until 10* (process + space + time) is far more likely than, say, *We spoke until 10 in the bar quietly.*

Subjuncts are adverbials which play a **subordinate** role to one of the other clause elements, or to the whole clause.

* In the sentence *Even Jim left early,* the adverb *even* is acting as a subjunct. It relates specifically to *Jim,* and not to the other words in the sentence.

* In the sentence *Would you sit here, please*? the adverb *please* is a subjunct, adding courtesy to the whole clause. It is not really contributing to the meaning of the clause in the same way that the other elements do.

Subjuncts therefore cannot be used within the clause in as full a range of contexts as can adjuncts. The two criteria for adjunct use on p.181 do not apply to subjuncts:

* We cannot focus on a subjunct:

  John certainly saw Jim.
  ~~It was certainly that John saw Jim.~~

* Nor can we use a subjunct to answer a question:

  How did John see Jim? ~~Certainly.~~

Types of subjunct

Subjuncts express a wide range of meanings.

- **Point of view**: *Morally, he should resign.* (i.e. from a moral point of view ...)

- **Courtesy**: *Kindly ask her to come in.*

- Expressing the **subject's attitude** towards the verb: *Reluctantly we walked home.*

- **Time**: *He's just left.   Are they still there?*

- **Emphasis**: *He really must leave.   Indeed she is.*

- **Increasing** the degree of intensity: *We know him well. I absolutely refuse to go.*

- **Decreasing** the degree of intensity: *She almost fell. I sort of agreed.   I only asked.*

- Attention **focusing**: *Even Fred could have done it. There were at least ten off work.*

Caution

Some adverbs can act either as subjuncts or as adjuncts. Compare the subjunct use in *Technically we can't go* (= from a technical point of view) and the adjunct use in *He spoke technically* (= in a technical manner).

Disjuncts are adverbials which play a **superior** role to the other elements in the clause. They act as if they were outside the clause, giving the speaker a chance to comment on what is taking place inside it, expressing speaker **stance**. There are two types:

- **Style** disjuncts convey the speaker's comment about the style or form of what is being said. They express the conditions under which the listener should interpret the accompanying sentence:

  Frankly, John should never have done it.
  (I tell you frankly that John should never have done it)

  Other style disjuncts include: *candidly, honestly, briefly, confidentially, literally, frankly speaking, to put it bluntly, so to say, if I may so put it.*

- **Content** disjuncts make an observation about the truth of the clause or a value judgment about its content:

  Fortunately, they remembered the key.

  Other content disjuncts include: *admittedly, indeed, most likely, doubtless, curiously, annoyingly, thankfully, of course, to our surprise, even more important.*

Disjuncts are little involved in the internal structure of the clause. The two criteria for adjunct use on p.181 do not apply to disjuncts:

- We cannot focus on a disjunct:

  In short, John saw Jim. ~~It was in short that John saw Jim~~.

- Nor can we use a subjunct to answer a question:

  How did John see Jim? ~~In short.~~

Usage

Many people object on stylistic grounds to the disjunct *hopefully* in such contexts as *Hopefully, sales will improve.* They argue that *hopefully* does not modify the verb in such cases (one cannot 'improve hopefully'), and that an alternative phrasing should be used, such as *It is hoped that ...* or *I hope that ...* It is unclear why this particular disjunct should have attracted so much adverse criticism, when many other disjuncts are used in a similar way: *thankfully, regrettably, sadly, happily,* etc.

'I'm warning you for the last time, Mac —
"Hopefully" is an adverb.'

Conjuncts are adverbials whose function is to relate (or 'conjoin') independent grammatical units, such as clauses, sentences, and paragraphs. They express a very different range of meanings from that found in the other adverbials.

Conjuncts are often used as essential linking items between the clauses and sentences of a narrative:

… **so** John asked me not to go. **However**, I'd made up my mind, and **as a result** I left for work as usual. **Meanwhile**, Fred had decided that he'd stay at home for a change – he's been feeling a lot better lately, **by the way** – and **so** when I got to the office …

Conjuncts are little involved in the internal structure of the clause. The two criteria for adjunct use on p.181 do not apply to conjuncts.

- We cannot focus on a conjunct:

  Nevertheless, John saw Jim.
  It was nevertheless that John saw Jim.

- Nor can we use a conjunct to answer a question:

  How did John see Jim? Nevertheless.

Conjuncts are often called 'sentence adverbs', but other types of adverbial can also modify sentences – disjuncts (p.184) and sentence adjuncts (p.180).

Types of conjunct

We can group conjuncts into seven main types, based on the kind of meaning they express.

- **Listing**: a large number of conjuncts can be used to build up a list, adding or enumerating extra information: *first, to begin with, secondly, likewise, furthermore, next, to conclude, last of all, finally, moreover.*

- **Summarising**: *all in all, to conclude, to sum up, overall.*

- **Same or similar meaning** (as in apposition, p.152): *in other words, namely, that is, for instance.*

- **Expressing result**: *therefore, consequently, as a result.*

- **Inferring**: *otherwise, in that case, else.*

- **Contrasting**: *rather, more precisely, in other words, on the other hand, alternatively, instead, however.*

- **Attention shifting**: *by the way, incidentally, meanwhile, in the meantime.*

Caution

Some words can appear either as conjuncts or as another type of adverbial, depending on how they are used.

Now, I'll tell you what to do. (conjunct)
Let's go **now.** (adjunct)

A **preposition** expresses a relationship of meaning between two parts of a sentence, most often showing how the two parts are related in space or time.

We ate **in** a restaurant.   She left **at** 3 o'clock.

The construction following the preposition is known as the **prepositional complement**. This is usually a noun phrase (p.112), but it can also be certain kinds of clause (p.83):

I'll take you **to** the bus stop. (noun phrase)
I'll take you **to** wherever you want. (clause)

The combination of a preposition with its complement is known as a **prepositional phrase**.

Prepositional phrases have three functions:

• They can be a **postmodifier** in the noun phrase (p.146):

I saw a man **in a raincoat**.

• They can be an **adverbial** (p.68):

In the morning, we went home.

• They can **complement** a verb or adjective (p.166):

He lay **on the floor**.   I'm sorry **for him**.

- Occasionally, a preposition may have an adjective or an adverb as its complement:

at last	by far	in brief	at worst
since when	in there	until now	before long

- A preposition may have a whole prepositional phrase as a complement. We then find two prepositions being used next to each other:

Come out **from under** the table.
It's warm everywhere **except in** the kitchen.

Caution

Finite clauses have to be introduced by a *wh-* word, like *what* or *who* (p.157), before they can be the complement of a preposition. Such clauses perform the same function as noun phrases:

He looked at **the answer**.
He looked at **what the answer was**.

These are very different from other subordinate clauses that are not like noun phrases:

He stopped **when the whistle blew**.

Here *when* is not a preposition, but a conjunction (p.204). Other words which can be both prepositions and conjunctions include *after*, *as*, *before*, *since* and *until*.

Most of the common prepositions consist of only one word: they are the **simple** prepositions. **Complex** prepositions consist of more than one word.

Simple prepositions include:

about, across, after, at, before, behind, by, down, during, for, from, in, inside, into, of, off, on, onto, out, over, round, since, through, to, toward(s), under, up, with

Complex prepositions containing two words include:

ahead of, apart from, because of, close to, due to, except for, instead of, near to

Complex prepositions containing three words include:

as far as, by means of, in accordance with, in addition to, in front of, in spite of, in terms of, on behalf of, with reference to

The words in a complex preposition do not vary freely, as they would in other circumstances. For example, *in spite of* cannot change to ~~out spite of~~, ~~in a spite of~~, or ~~in spite for~~.

Usage

Several prepositions are very restricted in their frequency or style, especially those which are recent borrowings from foreign languages: *anti, circa, pace, versus, vis-à-vis. Unto* is archaic, and used only in religious contexts. There are also several dialect uses: *towards* (British) vs. *toward* (American), *agin* (Scots, = 'against'), *outwith* (Scots, = 'except'), *while* (Yorkshire, = 'until').

Caution

* There are several words which can behave like prepositions, though they also show features of other word classes, such as verbs and adjectives (p.83). They are known as **marginal** prepositions.

  Granted his interest in fish, ...
  Considering your objections, ...
  Three **plus** three shouldn't be difficult.
  He's here **minus** his wife.

* Superficially, a three-word preposition, such as **in accordance with**, resembles a sequence of two noun phrases (p.112):

  He acted in **accordance** with **my instructions**.
  He went in **the bus** with **the red roof**.

  But *in accordance with* acts as a unit, whereas *in the bus with* does not. We can vary the latter in many different ways: *in the buses, on the bus, in the comfortable bus,* etc.

Caution

- From the above examples, it is evident that any one preposition may be used in several different ways. *Over*, for example, can be used in the sense of position (*The picture was over the door*), movement across (*They climbed over the wall*), accompanying circumstances (*We'll talk about it over dinner*), orientation to the speaker (*They live over the road*), and so on. *With* is another preposition with a wide range of meanings.

- Prepositions often have **figurative** as well as literal uses.

He's in a hole. (literally: in the ground)
He's in a hole. (figuratively: in trouble)

Likewise, *in the army, in uniform, in tears, in trouble, in a spot, in deep water,* and other such phrases all display meanings which are not literally 'in'. Most of these phrases have to be learned individually, as **idioms**.

"US and Soviet officials agreed on five adjectives to describe the meeting – interesting, useful, frank, businesslike, productive – but failed to agree on any prepositions."

Usage

- Normally, a preposition is followed directly by its complement. But in some cases this does not happen (the preposition is **deferred** or **stranded**):

Have they been paid **for**?
He's nice to be **with**.
She's worth listening **to**.

With *wh-* questions (p.49) and relative clauses (p.148), there is a choice between formal and informal usage:

Which book did you read from? (informal)
From which book did you read? (formal)

He's the man I was talking to. (informal)
He's the man to whom I was talking. (formal)

People often criticise the use of deferred prepositions in formal style: 'Never end a sentence with a preposition'. In some cases, however, there is no real alternative: *What did it look like?* (*Like what did it look?*)

- Prepositions are followed by the **objective** form of a pronoun (p.162): *to me*, not *to I*. But *than* is a problem, because there is conflict between two constructions. In *He's taller than me*, *than* acts as a preposition; whereas in *He's taller than I am*, it is a conjunction (p.208). However, there has long been a preference in traditional grammar for **subjective** pronouns (p.162), so that *He's taller than I* is frequently recommended as correct.

There are two main ways in which sentence structure can be shortened, to avoid saying or writing the same thing twice.

The use of 'pro-forms'

A **pro-form** is a word that is used to replace or refer to a longer construction in a sentence.

- A pro-form can **replace** a longer construction:

  I've got **a new car** and John's got **one** too.
  (John's got a new car too)

  When constructions are replaced in this way, the process is called pro-form **substitution**.

- A pro-form can be used to **refer** directly to a longer construction, which has the same meaning as the pro-form:

  Two people hurt **themselves** in the accident.

  Here, *themselves* does not replace *two people*, but simply refers back to it. *Two people hurt two people* ... would mean two **other** people. When the pro-form has the same meaning (or 'reference') as another construction, but does not replace it, we talk about pro-form **coreference**.

Reducing and expanding sentences

What can be a pro-form?

- Pro-forms used in coreference are usually **definite pronouns** (p.156): *she, they, myself, his, hers, this, those, such,* etc. We can also use a few **definite adverbs** of time or space (p.178): *then, there, here.*

- Pro-forms used in substitution can be either definite or indefinite. They are mostly **indefinite pronouns** (p.158): *one(s), some, none, either, few, many, several, all, both, another,* etc. We can also use a few adverbs (such as *so, thus, similarly*) and the verb *do,* either alone or in combination (*do so, do similarly,* etc.).

Most pro-forms replace or refer to some or all of a noun phrase (p.112). But a few other constructions are involved:

- The adverb pro-forms relate to adverbials (p.68):

  Fred walked to town and I went **there** too.

- *Do* relates to a part of the clause containing the verb (p.56):

  Fred walked to town and I **did** too.
  (where *did* replaces *walked to town*)

- *So* can replace an object, complement, or adverbial (p.44), or even a whole clause:

  A: John's leaving home. B: I told you **so**.
  (where *so* replaces all of the first clause)

Ellipsis

Ellipsis occurs when part of a sentence is left out because it would otherwise repeat what is said elsewhere.

I'd like to go to the cinema but I can't. ✗
I'd like to go to the cinema but I can't go to the cinema.

People usually find such repetitions unnecessary or boring, and use ellipsis to achieve a more acceptable economy of statement.

It is part of the definition of ellipsis that it should be absolutely obvious what the omitted words are: *go to the cinema*, in the above example. If it is unclear what has been omitted, we cannot call a sentence elliptical. Verbless constructions (p.168) also illustrate this condition.

A: Have another biscuit? B: Thanks.

Thanks cannot be called an elliptical sentence, because it is not 'short' for a longer sentence – as can be shown by asking what that longer sentence might be. There are many possibilities, and it is not possible to choose between them: *I give you thanks, My thanks are due to you, I owe you thanks for this biscuit, This humble person thanks you for the biscuit,* and so on.

The principle of being able to work out exactly what the omitted words are, by looking at the context, is called the principle of **recoverability**.

Types of recoverability

There are three kinds of recoverability:

- **Textual recoverability**: the full form of the sentence can be found by looking at the rest of the text: *Mike went by bus and later by train.* (i.e. Mike went by train).

- **Situational recoverability**: the full form of the sentence can be deduced by looking at the situation in which it was used: *Told you so*, where the choice of omitted subject (*I* or *we*) would be evident from the people present.

- **Structural recoverability**: the full form of the sentence can be found in the speaker's knowledge of grammar: in the headline, *PM to resign*, we can add *the* and *is* because we know how the language normally works.

Usage

- Situational ellipsis is very common in conversation:

  Want a drink?   Serves you right.   Looks like rain.
  Good to see you.   Anyone in?   You hungry?

- Ellipsis can refer forwards in the sentence (be **cataphoric**, p.138) as well as backwards (be **anaphoric**): *Don't ask me why, but the window is open.* However, some of these cases are not always wholly acceptable: *If you'll buy the white, I'll buy the red wine.*

Up to this point, most of the sentences illustrated in this book contain only one clause (p.41): they are **simple** sentences. Sentences which can be immediately analysed into more than one clause are **multiple** sentences. There are two types of multiple sentence: **compound** and **complex**.

Compound sentences

In compound sentences, the clauses are linked by **coordination** – usually, by the coordinators *and*, *or*, or *but* (p.204). Each clause could in principle stand as a sentence on its own (be an **independent**, or **main** clause):

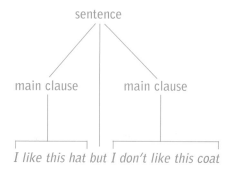

sentence

main clause   main clause

I like this hat but I don't like this coat

The same analysis is made even when one of the clauses has elements omitted due to ellipsis (p.198). In *I went by bus and Mary by train*, *Mary by train* can – once the ellipsis has been 'filled out' – stand as a main clause: *Mary went by train*.

Reducing and expanding sentences

Complex sentences

In complex sentences, the clauses are linked by **subordination**, using such words as *because*, *when*, and *although* (p.208). Here, one clause (the **subordinate clause**) is subordinated to another (the **main clause**).

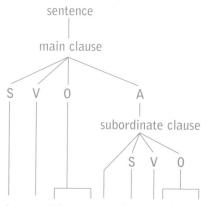

I answered the door when Jane rang the bell

The subordinate clause cannot stand as a sentence on its own. *When Jane rang the bell* needs some other clause before it can be used. The subordinate clause is often said to be 'embedded' in the main clause.

Caution

The subordinate clause always expands an element of main clause structure: all or part of the subject, object, complement, or adverbial (p.44). In the above, the main clause adverbial has been expanded. For examples of the other elements being expanded as clauses, see p.212.

Multiple structures

Both compound and complex sentences can contain several instances of coordination or subordination.

• With **multiple coordination**, the analysis is simple:

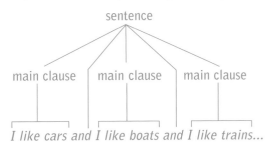

I like cars and I like boats and I like trains...

• With **multiple subordination**, we must take special care to keep the different 'levels' of subordination apart. In the next sentence, the first subordinate clause tells us what the speaker thought ('They will leave when the boat arrives'), and is therefore object of the verb *thought*. The second subordinate clause tells us when they would leave ('when the boat arrives'), and is an adverbial modifying *leave*.

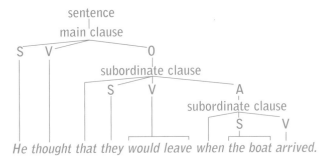

He thought that they would leave when the boat arrived.

Reducing and expanding sentences

- Several instances of subordination may occur 'at the same level'. In the following sentence, despite the apparent complexity, there is basically only a three-part structure, comparable to *That is that*:

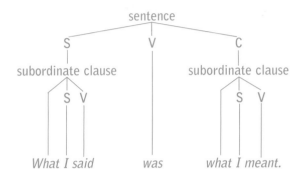

- Coordination and subordination may occur in the same sentence, to produce a **compound–complex** sentence:

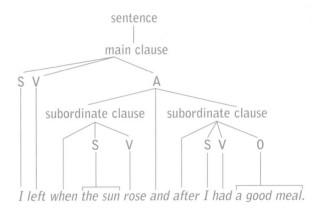

Sentences can be made bigger by joining clauses or parts of clauses together. But there are two distinct ways in which this can be done: through **coordination** and **subordination** (p.208).

Coordination

In coordination, the units that are joined have the same status in the sentence. For example, the two units could both be noun phrases (p.112), adjectives (p.166), or separate clauses (p.40):

I saw **a car** and **a bus**.   The kids were **wet** and **filthy**.
Mary went to York and **Hilary went to Leeds**.

Coordination with *and* could continue indefinitely: *They were wet and dirty and tired and happy and ...*

Coordination is usually signalled by a linking word, called a **coordinating conjunction** (or **coordinator**). The most common coordinators are *and, or,* and *but.* There are also a few 'pairs' of conjunctions (**correlatives**, such as *both ... and* and *(n)either ... (n)or*): *I spoke to (both) Hilary and Mary.*

These rules govern the use of clause coordinators:

- They must appear at the beginning of the clause:

  Hilary went to Leeds, **and** Mary went to York.
  ~~Hilary went to Leeds, Mary went to York **and**~~.

  This is a big difference between conjunctions and most **conjuncts** (p.186), which do have some mobility:

  Hilary went to Leeds; **however**, Mary went to York.
  Hilary went to Leeds; Mary went to York, **however**.

- A coordinated clause is fixed in relation to the previous clause, and cannot change places with it:

  Hilary went to Leeds, **but** Mary went to York.
  ~~**But** Mary went to York; Hilary went to Leeds.~~

  This is a big difference between coordinate clauses and most subordinate clauses (p.208):

  Hilary went to Leeds, **when** Mary went to York.
  When Mary went to York, Hilary went to Leeds.

- Coordinators cannot be preceded by another conjunction:

  ~~Hilary went to Leeds, **and but** Mary went to York~~.

  This is another way in which coordination differs from both conjuncts and subordination:

  Hilary went to Leeds; **and moreover** Mary went to York.
  Hilary went to Leeds; **and when** she arrived, Mary left.

Types of coordination

When a conjunction links two units, the coordination is said to
be **linked** (or **syndetic**). This is the more usual form. When
there is no conjunction, the coordination is **unlinked** (or
asyndetic). Both types are illustrated here:

The shop has **apples and oranges and pears**.
The shop has **apples, oranges, pears** – everything.

When two phrases are linked by *and*, they may express either
of two kinds of meaning.

- The two phrases combine to function as one unit of
  meaning, with reference to the rest of the clause
  (**combinatory** coordination). The unity can be shown by the
  way the phrases **cannot** be expanded into separate clauses:

  Hilary and Mary look alike.
  ~~Hilary looks alike and Mary looks alike~~.

- The two phrases retain their separate identities
  (**segregatory** coordination): each phrase can be
  expanded into its own clause:

  Hilary and Mary went to Leeds.
  Hilary went to Leeds and Mary went to Leeds.

  The adverb *respectively* is one way of showing segregatory
  meaning: *Hilary and Mary went to Leeds and York
  respectively.* This means that 'Hilary went to Leeds' and
  'Mary went to York'.

There are several idiomatic uses of *and*, especially common in informal speech, and often criticised in writing.

- In such constructions as *I'll try and see him* and *Why did you go and upset her?*, *and* is not a coordinator, but an informal equivalent of *to*: *I'll try to see him*.

- Likewise, in such constructions as *The room was nice and warm*, *nice and* is being used like an intensifying word (such as *very*), and not as a coordinator. Note also: *I drove it good and hard*, *well and truly drunk*, etc.

- By coordinating a word with itself, special meanings are expressed, such as intensification (*The car went slower and slower*) or continuous action (*They talked and talked*). Note also such uses as: *There are politicians and politicians*, meaning 'There are two kinds of politician'.

Caution

When a plural noun phrase contains modifiers (p.144) linked by *and*, there is always a risk of ambiguity. *Old men and women* could mean 'old men + old women' or 'old men + (any age) women'.

In subordination, the units that are joined together do not have the same grammatical status, as they do in the case of coordination (p.204). For example, one noun phrase can be made subordinate to another, by using it as a postmodifier (p.146):

The **dog** in that **kennel** looks fierce.

Here, *dog* is the 'main' noun – the **head** of the phrase – and *in that kennel* provides extra information about it.

Clause subordination

In the case of multiple sentences (p.200), one clause (known as the **subordinate**, **dependent**, or **embedded** clause) has been made to rely grammatically upon another (the **main** or **principal** clause). As a result, the information it contains is placed in the background, compared with the information expressed by the main clause.

Subordination is usually signalled by a linking word, called a **subordinating conjunction** (or **subordinator**). There are many subordinators, expressing a wide range of meanings. They are illustrated on p.213.

Markers of subordination

Most subordinate clauses are signalled by the use of a subordinating conjunction. There are three main types:

- **simple** subordinators consist of one word:
  although, if, since, that, unless, until, whereas, while, etc.

- **complex** subordinators consist of more than one word:
  in order that, such that, granted (that), assuming (that), so (that), as long as, insofar as, in case, etc.

- **correlative** subordinators consist of 'pairs' of words which relate two parts of the sentence:
  as ... so ..., scarcely ... when ..., if ... then ..., etc.

  As the sun went down, **so** the crying stopped.
  I was **more** interested **than** he had been.
  The further they walked, **the** angrier they became.

In a few cases, subordination can be signalled without a subordinating conjunction:

- *Wh-* words and *that* mark a relative clause as subordinate (p.148): *The man who left was ill*.

- The inversion of subject and verb can signal subordination (though this usage is literary or formal): *Were she here, she would tell you*.

- Comment clauses, such as *you know* (p.214), are always subordinate, though they have no grammatical subordination marker at all.

The functions of subordinate clauses

Subordinate clauses can replace the whole of any clause element except the verb (p.57). Their grammatical function can always be tested by replacing the clause with a simpler unit, such as a pronoun, adjective, adverb, or noun phrase.

* **Subject** (p.60):

  That he didn't arrive on time is awful.
  (compare: **This** is awful)

* **Object** (p.62), both direct and indirect:

  Tony doesn't know **what to do**.
  (compare: He doesn't know **something**)

  Give it to **whoever is outside**.
  (compare: Give it to **him**)

* **Complement** (p.64), both subject and object:

  The results are **what I expected**.
  (compare: They are **interesting**)

  I find Jimmy **to be someone I can trust**.
  (compare: I find him **trustworthy**)

* **Adverbial** (p.68):

  Show me the photos **when you next visit us**.
  (compare: Show me them **then**)

Clauses which expand subject, object, and complement elements (where noun phrases function) are sometimes called **noun clauses**.

Caution

There are also three cases where a subordinate clause may appear as **part** of a clause element, and these should be carefully distinguished from those where the clause acts as a **whole** element (see facing page):

- as a **postmodifier** in the noun phrase (p.146):

  I saw the man **who sent me a letter**.

- as the **complement to a preposition** (p.188):

  It depends on **how you start**.

- as the **complement to an adjective** (p.166):

  We were happy **to start climbing the wall**.

In each case, if the subordinate clause were taken away, there would be some part of the clause element remaining: *the man*, *on*, and *happy*, respectively.

There is therefore a clear contrast between the following two sentences:

I know **which he chose**.
I know **the books which he chose**.

In the first case, *which he chose* forms the whole of the object element; in the second case, it is only part of that element.

Coordinator meanings

- *And* often expresses a very general meaning of **addition** (*He drives a car and he rides a bike*), where the reverse order is acceptable (*He rides a bike and he drives a car*).

  And can also convey a number of specific nuances, such as **result** (*I worked hard and (therefore) passed the exam*) or **time sequence** (*I got up and (then) I went out*), and here reverse order is unacceptable (*I went out and I got up*).

- *Or* introduces an **alternative**. Usually, the alternatives are taken to exclude each other, as when *You can eat now or later* means 'eat now or later but not both'. This is known as **exclusive *or***.

  Inclusive interpretations also occur, where *or* approaches the meaning of *and*: *You can eat now or later – I don't mind which*.

- *But* always expresses a **contrast** in meaning: *I got to the station by 3, but the train had already gone*.

  It is unusual to find more than one instance of *but* in a sentence, and such cases are often considered to be stylistically inelegant:

  I got there by 3 but the train had gone but there was another one an hour later.

212

Subordinator meanings

Subordinators express a much wider range of meaning than coordinators, especially in signalling **adverbial** clauses (p.210). Some of the common meanings and subordinators used in adverbial clauses are given below.

Meanings	Subordinators	Examples
time	*after, as, before, since, till, until, when, while*	I arrived **while you were out**.
place	*where, wherever*	I see **where he is**.
condition	*if, unless, in case, as long as, supposing*	I'll go **if you come with me**.
concession	*although, though, if, even if, whereas*	I played, **though I was hurt**.
contrast	*whereas, while, whilst*	I sing, **whereas you don't**.
exception	*except, but that, save that, excepting that*	I'd go, **except that I've no money**.
reason	*because, since, for, as*	I can't go, **because it's expensive**.
purpose	*to, in order to, so as to*	I left early, **to get the train**.
result	*so, so that*	He was tired, **so he went to bed**.
similarity	*as, like*	Do **as I say**.
comparison	*as if, as though, like*	It looks **as if he's in**
proportion	*as ... so, the ... the*	**The** more I do, **the** less I like it.
preference	*rather than, sooner than*	I'd walk, **rather than go on a horse**.

Comment clauses give speakers an opportunity to express their attitude about what they are saying or the way they are saying it (as do adverbial disjuncts, p.184). They are particularly common in informal conversation, where they are often spoken in a parenthetic tone of voice, with increased speed and decreased loudness.

Everything else, **I imagine**, will arrive on Monday.
You see, he always was a clever chap.
That seems very sensible, **I must say**.

Comment clause meanings

Comment clauses express quite a wide range of meanings, such as the following:

• **Tentativeness**: *I think, I assume, I suppose, I'm told, they say, it's rumoured, it seems.*

• **Certainty**: *I know, I'm sure, it transpires, I must say, I've no doubt, it's true.*

• **Specific emotional attitude**: *I'm glad to say, I'm afraid, I hope, Heaven knows.*

• **Asking for attention**: *you know, you see, mind you, you must admit, as you may have heard.*

Types of comment clause

All the comment clauses illustrated above have the basic structure of a main clause: they contain a subject and a verb (*you know, it seems*), though they lack the other elements which these verbs normally require (*you know something, it seems that ...*). Several other types of comment clause display a different kind of structure:

- **adverbial** clauses (p.210) beginning with *as*: *as you know, as it happens, as I've said*, etc.

- **relative** clauses (p.148) beginning with *what*: *what is more, what annoys me, what's very strange*, etc.

- nonfinite clauses (p.83) beginning with an **infinitive** with *to*: *to be fair, to be honest, to put it bluntly*, etc.

- nonfinite clauses containing an **-ing participle** (p.78): *roughly speaking, putting it bluntly*, etc.

- nonfinite clauses beginning with an **-ed participle** (p.79): *put plainly, stated in words of one syllable*, etc.

Usage

Comment clauses are important features of conversation, as they help speakers to 'think on their feet' and give listeners a chance to grasp what is being said. But their over-use is widely held to be a sign of unclear thinking.

Comparative clauses express a comparison in respect of some standard.

My castle is bigger than Arthur's castle (is).

Here, the meaning of the subordinate clause (p.208), *than Arthur's castle (is)*, is compared with the meaning expressed by the subject, *my castle*, with respect to the standard of 'size'.

In a broad sense, comparison includes a range of meanings, such as excess, sufficiency, and equivalence:

You're going too far. (excess)
He had walked far enough. (sufficiency)
She's as tall as her mother. (equivalence)

In a narrower sense, comparison involves the measurement of different degrees of **nonequivalence** – something being 'more' or 'less' than something else. This is expressed by a construction which relates two parts of the sentence (a **correlative** construction). The first part makes use of a **comparative element**, involving *more*, *less*, or a word ending (*-er*, *-est*) (p.172). The second part consists of a subordinate clause preceded by *than*.

I'm **taller / than you**.   He's **more curious / than I am**.

Reducing and expanding sentences

Caution

The comparative clause is especially interesting because it is constructed in a unique way, and it is not obvious how best to analyse it. One analysis looks like this:

John is happier than Bill is.
S V   C   A

The comparative element *happier* is analysed as a complement (p.64), and the subordinate clause as an adverbial. However, this raises problems. The analysis does not reflect the feeling we have that the *-er* and *than* 'go together'. No other adverbial clause depends on a complement element in this way.

An alternative analysis, which keeps these elements together, looks like this:

John is **happier than Bill is**.
S V   C

Here, *happier* is seen as the head of the complement element, with the *than-* clause acting as a kind of postmodification (p.146).

The same analysis would be made for other kinds of comparative construction:

John is **less involved than Bill is**.
S V   C

John is **as involved as Bill is**.
S V   C

The usual way in which we report someone's speech is by using a special **reporting clause**, such as *She said, He wrote, They replied* – sometimes adding extra information (*She said angrily, He wrote with a flourish*).

The accompanying speech or writing is given in the **reported clause**. This clause appears in two forms:

• **Direct speech** gives the exact words used by the speaker or writer. They are usually enclosed by quotation marks (but see pp. 221, 237).

Michael said, 'I am not interested.'

• **Indirect speech** gives the words as subsequently reported by someone. It usually takes the form of a subordinate clause (p.208) introduced by *that*.

Michael said that he was not interested.

Caution

Older grammars refer to these two modes as **oratio recta** (for direct speech) and **oratio obliqua** (for indirect speech). Indirect speech is also often call **reported speech**.

Grammatical differences

When indirect speech is used, speakers need to change the wording to allow for differences between their current situation and the situation they are reporting.

* **Tense** forms (p.100): it is usually necessary to change the tense form of the verbs used in the direct speech. In most cases, the present tense becomes past, and the past tense is shifted still further back, by using the perfective aspect (p.104). The correct relationship between the verbs in the reporting and reported clauses is known as the **sequence of tenses**.

  He said, 'I **am** staying in London.'
  He said that he **was** staying in London.
  He said, 'I **walked** to London.'
  He said that he **had walked** to London.

* **Time** and **place** references: *tomorrow* becomes *the next day*, *here* becomes *there*, etc.

  He said, 'I saw it **here yesterday**.'
  He said he'd seen it **there the day before**.

* **Personal pronouns** (p.160): first and second person pronouns have to be changed to third person, unless the original participants are still involved in the conversation:

  Mary said to John, 'I saw **your** cat.'
  Mary said that **she** had seen **his** cat.
  Mary said that **she'd** seen **your** cat. (if the reporter is talking to John)

Special uses in literature

The basic distinction between direct
and indirect speech often appears in
a modified form in literature. There
are two main styles, illustrated below
from a translation of Alexander
Solzhenitsyn's *Cancer Ward*.

* **Free indirect speech** is mainly used when an author is
  representing a stream of thought. It is basically indirect
  speech, as is shown by the changes in tense forms (p.219).
  But there is no reporting clause, and several features of
  direct speech are retained (such as exclamations, p.54):

> He wrapped up his neck and sat down by the wall. How
> dumb they all **were**, how submissive, wooden almost! Except
> for Azovkin nobody really **looked** as if he **was** suffering.
> They **were** not really worthy of recovery.

* **Free direct speech** can also represent a stream of thought.
  It is basically a form of direct speech, as shown by the
  present-tense forms; but there is no reporting clause to mark
  the change from past-tense narrative:

> It was a dampish chilly morning, but not wintry. People
> **would** be wearing raincoats on a day like that back in
> Central Russia, but **here** in the south people **have** different
> ideas of hot and cold.

- The reporting clause may occur before, within, or after an instance of direct speech. When it occurs in the middle or at the end of the sentence, the order of subject and verb can sometimes be inverted:

'I think,' Michael said, 'that we should go.'
'I think,' said Michael, 'that we should go.'

The inversion is commonest when the verb is *said*, and the subject is not a pronoun (p.154). *Said he* is literary or archaic, and forms such as ~~laughed she~~ or ~~complained they~~ are unacceptable.

- Inversion at the beginning of a sentence is found only in some styles of journalism: *Declared red-haired Tracey: 'I love him deeply.'*

- The *that* used before a reported clause is often omitted in informal contexts: *John said he had seen her before.*

> When conversation is being represented in fiction, the reporting clause is often omitted, if the identity of the speakers would be clear from the context. Quotation marks are also sometimes omitted. In drama, the verb of the reporting clause is always omitted, and quotation marks are never used:
>
> FRED: (angrily) But did you do it?
> MARY: Of course not.

There are many ways in which we can organise the information contained in a sentence, as can be seen from these alternatives:

A dog was chasing a cat.
There was a dog chasing a cat.
It was a dog that was chasing a cat.
A cat was being chased by a dog.

These sentences all express the same meaning, but they convey several important differences of style and emphasis. Analysis of these differences is also part of the study of grammar.

Prosody

It is difficult to convey all aspects of spoken emphasis by writing examples down. In speech, a great deal of meaning is signalled by varying our pitch, loudness, and other such features (**prosody**, p.236). In particular, meaning can be altered by making one word in a construction more prominent than the others. These words are printed in SMALL CAPITALS in chapters 70–72.

I have a BIG dog. (not a little one)

Given and new information

There are usually two kinds of information in a sentence. One part of the sentence tells us something **new**. The other part tells us something that we were aware of already (either from previous sentences or from our general knowledge) – in other words, its information is **given**. The distinction between given and new information can be clearly seen in this dialogue:

A: Where did **you leave the car**?
B: I left the car / outside the STATION.
   Given   **New**

Theme and focus

- Given information tells us what a sentence is about; it provides the sentence **theme**. Because the information it contains is familiar, this part of the sentence is not likely to be spoken with extra prominence.

- New information provides the point where we expect people to pay special attention, or **focus**. The part of the sentence containing the focus is always spoken in a prominent way.

In most sentences, the theme appears first, and the focus of the message last. But it is possible to bring the focus forwards, so as to emphasise an earlier part of the sentence. This especially happens when we want to state a contrast, as in *The TABLE's broken, not the chair*. It also happens when the information in the second part of the sentence is predictable, as in *The SUN's shining*.

There are several ways in which special attention can be drawn to the theme of a sentence.

Fronting

Fronting occurs when we move to the beginning of a sentence an item which does not usually belong there. This item then becomes the theme, but it carries extra prominence:

BLOGGS–BRIGGS I said my name was.
INTO THE SEA they dived.
A WELSHMAN I was born, and A WELSHMAN I shall die.

Inversion

Inversion involves the subject and verb appearing in the reverse of their normal order:

Here's the POSTMAN.   Down **came the** RAIN.
In a distant country **lies my dearest** FRIEND.
She was angry and so **was** I.

The verbs must be in their simple forms (p.106): we cannot say ~~Down was coming the RAIN~~, etc.

Cleft sentences

Another way of altering the normal emphasis in a simple sentence is to split the sentence into two clauses, giving each its own verb. The first clause consists of the pronoun *it* (with no meaning, p.161) and a form of the verb *be*. The second clause begins with a pronoun such as *that* or *who*. These constructions are called **cleft sentences**:

John kicked the ball into the goal.
It was JOHN who kicked the ball into the goal.

Other parts of the sentence can be focused in this way:

It was THE GOAL that John kicked the ball into.
It was THE BALL that John kicked into the goal.

Extraposition

Where the subject or object element is a clause (p.60), it is possible to change the sentence around so that the clause comes later. The element is then replaced by the pronoun *it*, which 'anticipates' the following clause:

What you say doesn't matter.
It doesn't matter **what you say**.

I find **working here** a bore.
I find **it** a bore, **working here**.

In examples like these, the clauses have been moved **outside of** their normal position in the sentence. The effect is thus said to be one of **extraposition**.

Sometimes we want to bring the content of a **whole** clause to the attention of our listener or reader, as new information (p.223). To do this, we can use a construction in which the first words have no meaning. They seem to act as a theme, because they appear at the beginning of the sentence (p.223); but it is an 'empty' or 'dummy' theme.

The main means of achieving this effect is to use the word *there* followed by the simple present or past tense of *be*:

Many animals are in DANGER these days.
There are many animals in DANGER these days.

These sentences express the general existence of some state of affairs. They are therefore called **existential** sentences.

Caution

This use of *there* is totally different from *there* used as an adverb of place. It has no locative meaning, as can be seen by the contrast: *There's a sheep over* THERE. Also, existential *there* carries no emphasis at all, whereas the adverb does: THERE *he is*.

Usage

There occurs in the position normally taken up by the subject of a clause (p.60). In informal speech, it often influences the form of the verb, causing singular concord (p.74) even where the verb is followed by a plural:

No, no, it's 'There are some apples on the table'...

There's some apples on the table.

This usage would be criticised in writing, or in formal speech, where *There are some apples on the table* would be recommended.

- *Be* is not the only verb capable of being used in an existential way, but the others are much rarer and more literary:

  There **exist** several variations of this proposal.
  There **arose** a great uproar.
  Soon after, there **occurred** a fresh development.

- There are several other ways of altering the emphasis of a sentence in colloquial speech. One way is simply to repeat a word (*It's much much too expensive*). Another is to add a phrase or clause as a 'tag' at the end of a sentence: *I don't trust him, your Fred; He likes a drink, Sid does*. In some northern British dialects, the subject and verb are inverted: *He likes a drink, does Sid*.

In real life, a sentence is rarely used in isolation. Normally, sentences – whether spoken or written – appear in a sequence, such as a dialogue, a speech, a letter, or a book. Any set of sentences which 'cohere' in this way is called a **text**. The coherence is achieved through the use of a wide range of features which **connect** sentences – features of general knowledge, vocabulary, punctuation (p.238), prosody (p.236), and – to some extent – grammar.

Caution

- In everyday use, the term **text** is restricted to pieces of written language. In the special language of linguistics, however, it refers to either spoken or written material.

- A text is a coherent, complete unit of speech or writing. As such, it typically consists of many sentences. But it is possible to find a text which contains only **one** sentence, as the picture shows.

DANGER

Types of connective feature

Several of the links between sentences have nothing to do with the grammar in which they are formulated.

- **General implications**: we often make a link between sentences because of our general knowledge or expectations.

  The summer was long and hot. The vintage was superb.

  Here there is no obvious connection in either grammar or vocabulary to link these sentences. But anyone who knows about wine can readily supply the missing link.

- **Vocabulary**: often the choice of words is enough to connect two sentences:

  Look at that Mercedes. What a car!

  Because the words *car* and *Mercedes* are clearly related in meaning, we have no difficulty making a connection.

- **Punctuation** and **layout** (or, in speech, **prosody**, p.236) may be enough to show that sentences – or even paragraphs – are to be connected in a specific way. The use of graphic sub-divisions within a text, to show how the meaning is organised, provides a clear example – as on the present page.

Grammatical connectivity

Several aspects of grammar, already discussed with reference
to sentence structure, can also be used to connect sentences.
They include:

- **Space and time adverbials** (p.178)
  We left at 5. **An hour later**, we were there.
  I increased speed. **Further on**, I passed John.

- **Pro-forms** (p.196)
  The Browns said they would pay us a visit. Whenever
  they **did so**, there was always a row.

- **Personal pronouns** (p.160)
  The children arrived early. **They** were tired.

- **Determiners** (p.136): *the/this/these/that/those*
  A scruffy boy appeared in the doorway. **The** boy was
  obviously hungry.

- **Comparison** (p.172)
  Six of us competed. Jack was **fastest**.

- **Conjunctions** (p.204)
  Several people complained. **But** I simply cannot take this
  matter seriously.

- **Conjuncts** (p.186)
  I have several points to discuss. **To begin with**, there's
  the question of money.

Words and phrases whose primary purpose is to connect clauses, sentences, and other large units of text are sometimes referred to as **connectives.**

> Several forms mark identity between what is being said and some aspect of what has been said before or is about to be said. They include *above, the following, the former, here,* etc. This kind of linkage is known as **discourse reference**.
>
> The crime rate is continuing to rise. **It**'s a national scandal.
>
> I'd like to make **the following** points. First, we need to encourage investment ...

Tracing connections between sentences

Often several features of connectivity are present to link a pair of sentences, and in a longer passage, the different links combine and overlap in many ways. This can be seen in the following paragraph, where the grammatical connections are highlighted.

> Mary and I started out at about nine in the morning. **Three hours later**, **we** reached the foot of Cook Mountain. Neither of **us** was used to climbing, so **we** slowed down considerably. **But** it was **easier** once we got near **the summit**. **And** there was a marvellous view, which made all **our** efforts seem worthwhile. Mary took several photos of **the** view. 'It's to prove **we** got **there**,' she remarked. 'I've got **better** proof than **that**,' I thought ruefully, looking down at my sore feet.

Sentences are the ways in which we organize what we want to say into intelligible units. Sentences, literally, 'make' sense. That is why it is necessary to study their structure in detail, for each individual grammatical feature makes available a contrast of meaning, and the more we are aware of what these contrasts are, can control them in our own expression, and can respond to them in the expression of others, the more we can develop a mature and confident command of English.

To achieve that goal, one final step needs to be taken. We need to move from sentence to text. We do not speak or write only in individual sentences. Sentences combine into sequences which form larger units of communication, variously called 'discourses' or 'texts'. Some texts have a determinate character imposed by constraints of time, space, genre, or technology: examples are news reporting, advertising, sports commentary, and text messaging. Others have no predictable direction or limit: examples include conversation and chatroom interaction. But in all cases, we are dealing with a linguistic reality where the overall communicative effect – what is usually referred to as 'style' – arises out of the combined use of many grammatical features, spread over several sentences.

The chief factor governing the selection of features which contribute to a style is **consistency**. If a style is inconsistent, or unpredictable, we are unable to locate it in our mental map of language varieties and evaluate it or respond to it appropriately. Inconsistency can appear in the use of any aspect of language structure – we can see it, for example, when people switch between formal and colloquial vocabulary, or between American and British spelling – but one of the most notable signs of an immature style is the inconsistent use of features of grammar. In the following pages, numbers in parentheses refer to earlier chapters in this book where a particular point of grammatical usage is outlined.

Avoiding inconsistency

To avoid inconsistency, we need to be aware of the nature of the semantic or pragmatic contrasts which the grammatical features convey. While this is the subject-matter of *Making Sense of Grammar* (p.253), the point can be briefly illustrated here with formality variation.

Consistency

Several grammatical features express a contrast between formal and informal style (pp.31–2). If the situation is one which motivates informality, we would expect clusters of informal usages, such as loosely coordinated sentences (1, 64), abbreviated or contracted forms (18, 62), interpolated comments (67), phrasal idioms (21), deictic reference (21), and deferred prepositions (61):

I think **yeah** that's what we should ask **for** – cos if we do**n't get a move on** there'**ll** be no time left to do anything – **and I mean it's** Friday already **and** most of the tickets'**ll** be gone **by now anyway** ...

Conversely, if the situation is one which motivates formality, we would expect clusters of formal usages, such as subordinate clause sequences (65), complex noun phrases (39, 40), uncontracted forms (18), prepositions attached to pronouns (61), and passive verbs (22):

It **is expected** that **the unusual pattern of expenditure**, **noted** in the audited accounts for 2002, is one **to which** board members are **expected** to pay special attention **when they meet in November.**

Literary prose

These are the opening lines of Charles Dickens' short story for Christmas, 'The Haunted Man':

Everybody said so.

Far be it from me to assert that what everybody says must be true. Everybody is, often, as likely to be wrong as right. In the general experience, everybody has been wrong so often, and it has taken in most instances such a weary while to find out how wrong, that the authority is proved to be fallible. Everybody may sometimes be right; 'but that's no rule,' as the ghost of Giles Scroggins says in the ballad.

The dread word, GHOST, recalls me.

Everybody said he looked like a haunted man. The extent of my present claim for everybody is, that they were so far right. He did.

Who could have seen his hollow cheek, his sunken brilliant eye; his black attired figure, indefinably grim, although well-knit and well-proportioned; his grizzled hair hanging, like tangled sea-weed about his face, – as if he had been, through his whole life, a lonely mark for the chafing and beating of the great deep of humanity, – but might have said he looked like a haunted man? Who could have observed his manner, taciturn, thoughtful, gloomy, shadowed by habitual reserve, retiring always and jocund never, with a distraught air of reverting to a bygone place and time, or of listening to some old echoes in his mind, but might have said it was the manner of a haunted man?

Who could have heard his voice, slow-speaking, deep, and grave, with a natural fulness and melody in wit which he seemed to set himself against and stop, but might have said it was the voice of a haunted man?

Anyone reading this passage will be struck by the controlled articulation of the writing, a certain liveliness of touch, the detailed character description, the varying narrative perspective, an immediate involvement in the story, and a growing sense of expectation – all effects largely controlled by the grammar.

- Opening with a pro-form (*so*) involves the reader (62). We do not know what the author is referring to, so we read on in order to find out. Dickens does it again in paragraph 4, where *he* is mentioned. We do not find out who 'he' is for another four pages.
- Liveliness is partly conveyed by altering the pace and rhythm of the reading through the alternation of long and short units. The second paragraph is bounded by two one-line paragraphs, and the fourth paragraph follows up two complex sentences with a contrasting two-word ellipsis (62, 63).
- Language play also adds to lightness of touch – here seen in the way the indefinite compound pronoun *everybody* is given a very definite, personalizing force (44).
- The accumulation of descriptive detail is achieved by exploiting the expressive potential of complex noun phrases, especially by the simultaneous use of premodifying and postmodifying adjectives and adjective phrases (39, 40, 48).
- The unusual use of postmodifying adjectives (40) adds atmosphere: compare what we have with the less dramatic effect conveyed by *his taciturn, thoughtful, gloomy manner*.
- Tenses control the narrative perspective – from past time (*said*) to current observation (*is, has been*) to past description (*said, were*) to background comment (*as if he had been...*) – to modal reflection (*could have*) (23, 24, 26).
- Elegant structuring is seen especially in the parallelism of the last three paragraphs (73). Each takes the form of a rhetorical question (5) with a symmetrical thematic opening and conclusion incorporating a set of variations (*Who could have seen ... observed ... heard ...*). The repeated questions increase our sense of anticipation.
- Notable also is the rhythmical balance of the coordinated adjective sequences (64), using pairs (*sunken brilliant*) and triads (*taciturn, thoughtful, gloomy*). There is parallelism within parallelism, as in *retiring always and jocund never*.

Web news reporting

This is the first part of a journalistic report in the style of a news page at a Web site, with pseudonyms replacing the real proper names. The narrow column width of the top few lines is due to an adjacent picture, not shown here.

Two hurt in raid on Illyrian terrorist camp

Two Tamasa rebels have been killed in a fierce gun battle which broke out after several Illyrian tanks, backed by helicopter gunships, raided a Matu River refugee camp.

Two boys aged eight and 14 were among those killed in the fighting in the Matu camp, which lies near the Illyrian northern capital of Ashaka, Tamasa medical sources said.

The Illyrian army say that their troops went in to uncover and destroy tunnels used for smuggling weapons from across the nearby border.

The incursion comes as the Tamasa leadership faces a new crisis amid reports that Prime Minister Shalema Maneshi has threatened to resign just two days after being sworn in.

Extensive search

Tamasa witnesses in Matu said that the Illyrian troops entered the camp from two different directions shortly after midnight (2200 GMT) and exchanges of fire with Tamasa gunmen swiftly began.

The gun battle continued after daybreak, witnesses said.

The semantic constraints on grammar are the same as in any kind of journalism, but the pragmatic constraints imposed by pressure on space and the need for screen legibility radically affect some of the grammatical choices made (pp.34–5).

- A large-type elliptical headline attracts attention (2, 62).
- Single-sentence paragraphs, separated by a line of white space, aid legibility. Paragraphs with two or three short sentences are possible, but unusual.
- The short sentence length helps information processing. It is rare to have sentences over 30 words, and much shorter sentences are common – in this example, one of eight words.
- The combination of these two factors here results in an 8-word paragraph, which would be unacceptable (unless a dramatic contrast were being made) in most styles of writing.
- The pressure on space and legibility demands a style which is highly compressed, motivating the use of subordinate clauses (65). The succinctness of the opening paragraph is not because the grammar is simple: on the contrary, the noun *battle* is followed by a relative clause (*which broke out...*) which contains an adverbial clause of time (*after several...*) which contains a nonfinite clause (*backed by...*) (17, 41, 54).
- The same pressure motivates the use of premodifiers in the noun phrase (39): in the first paragraph, *two Tamasa rebels, a fierce gun battle, a Matu River refugee camp*. Notice the increase in length which would result if postmodification had been used: *a camp for refugees by the Matu River.*
- The active voice is normal, but the passive is used in the first two paragraphs because the identity of the agent is unclear (22). Who exactly killed the rebels?
- Postmodifications add extra descriptive detail (40), as in paragraph 2: *aged eight and 14, in the Matu camp, of Ashaka.*
- Appositions (42) also add detail in a compact way: *Prime Minister Shalema Maneshi, midnight (2200 GMT).*
- The lack of quotation marks for direct speech in paragraphs 2 and 6 reduces graphic complexity (a common practice in journalism). The placement of the reporting clause (*said*) varies, to avoid an unduly repetitive style (69, 77).

The field of **word-formation** is marginal to grammar. It studies the principles which govern the construction of the thousands of words (or **lexical items**) in a language.

The parts of a word

- Many words cannot be broken down into grammatical parts (*boy, yes, person*). These consist only of a **base** form.

- Many words consist of a base form plus an **ending** whose only role is grammatical: it shows how the word must be used in a sentence, and it has no separate meaning. These are the **inflectional suffixes** (e.g. plural *-s* (p.122), past tense *-ed* (p.100), comparative *-er* (p.172).

- Many words consist of a base form plus an ending which **does** change the word's meaning (e.g. *-ness, -ship, -able*). These are the **derivational suffixes**.

- Many words consist of a base form plus a meaningful element which is attached before it (a **prefix**): *un-, de-, anti-*, etc.

This chapter corresponds to Chapter 74 in *Making Sense of Grammar* (see p.253).

Related issues

Prefixes and suffixes are often both used along with a base form.

un drink able   de central iz ation

Types of word-formation

There are four main ways of forming words, and a few less common ways. (Further examples of the first two types are given on pp.95, 117, 167, and 175.)

- **Prefixation**: putting a prefix in front of the base form.

  untie, **dis**obey, **post**war, **tri**cycle, **ex**-husband

- **Suffixation:** putting a suffix after the base form.

  boy**hood**, lion**ess**, kind**ness**, help**ful**, slow**ly**

- **Conversion**: changing a word from one word class to another, without an ending:

  Time to **down** tools. (adverb used as a verb)
  That book is a **must**. (verb used as a noun)

- **Compounding**: joining two bases, the first of which identifies an essential feature of the second: *armchair* (= a chair with arms), *chewing gum* (= gum for chewing).

Minor types of word-formation

* **Reduplication**: using a form twice, usually with a slight alteration: *higgledy-piggledy*, *goody-goody*, *bow-wow*, *tick-tock*.

* **Abbreviation**: shortening a word, either by omitting syllables (**clippings**, as in *ad*, *demo*, *pub*), using initial letters (**acronyms**, as in *VIP*, *TV*, *radar*), and joining parts of two words (**blends**, as in *breathalyser* and *Eurovision*).

Caution

* There is great inconsistency about how compound words are written. Some are written as single words, some as separate words, and some are hyphenated. Often usage is divided: we will find *flower pot*, *flower-pot*, and *flowerpot*. However, when a compound becomes established as a single word, it tends to be written without space or hyphen. Hyphenation is in any case less common in American than in British English.

* Compound words usually have a single main stress. This is enough to distinguish a *blackbird* (= a particular species) from a *black bird* (= a bird of any species which happens to be black), or a *hot-dog* (= a kind of food) from a *hot dog* (= a warm animal).

Morphology and syntax

The field of grammar is often divided into two main areas, one dealing with the analysis of words, the other with the analysis of sentences. The study of word structure is called **morphology**, and the study of sentence structure is called **syntax**.

Grammar

Morphology
(The structure of words)

Syntax
(The structure of sentences)

English makes little use of word structure to express grammatical meanings. Prefixes are not used in this way, and there are less than a dozen types of suffix which act as inflections (p.232). As a result, most of the information in this book has been about syntax.

The inflections of English

noun plural (p.122)	genitive *'s* (p.132)
past tense (p.100)	third person (p.78)
objective pronoun (p.162)	negative *n't* (p.85)
-ing participle (p.78)	*-ed* participle (p.79)
-er comparison (p.172)	*-est* comparison (p.172)
contracted forms of verbs (*'re*, *'ll*, etc.) (p.85)	

The study of the inflections used in a grammar was known as **accidence**, in older approaches. This has now been replaced by p.241 the study of morphology, which analyses words into their smallest meaningful elements (*morphemes.*)

Prosody refers to meaningful variations in the **loudness**, **pitch**, **speed**, and **rhythm** of speech. These variations need to be referred to in a grammar because they often influence the way sentence structure is analysed. They act, in effect, as the 'punctuation' of speech.

Most of the important variations fall into two types:

- **Intonation** is the use of pitch to express meaning. Our intonation conveys information about our emotions (anger, surprise, etc.) as well as about grammar.

- **Stress** is the use especially of loudness to make a word, or part of a word, stand out from the rest.

Intonation and stress often combine to make one part of the sentence more **prominent** than another.

Caution

In the vast majority of cases, the stress pattern of a word is fixed. But there are several instances where a change in the language is taking place, and the newer patterns usually attract criticism until they become established. Thus in Britain we find _controversy_ and (newer) _controversy_, a _disPUTE_ and (newer) _DISpute_, etc.

This chapter corresponds to Chapter 75 in _Making Sense of Grammar_ (see p.253).

Prosodic signals of two grammatical differences

- If someone is reciting a list of items, we know whether the list is complete or not by the pitch of the voice. If the pitch is rising (shown by ´), there are more items to come. If it is falling (shown by `), there is nothing further to come. The difference is suggested in writing by the use of a series of dots instead of a full stop (p.239):

I bought beer, whiskey, gín ... I bought beer, whiskey, gìn.

- The two types of **relative clause** (p.148) can be distinguished by intonation:

My BROTHER / who's ABROAD / has written to me.
(I have only one brother, and he's abroad)
My brother who's ABROAD / has written to me.
(my brother who's in LONDON / has not)

Usage

Failing to notice intonation or stress is a common reason for usage arguments. For example, in writing, it is wise to place *only* next to the word it modifies, otherwise there may be ambiguity. The context usually makes the meaning clear, but in theory a sentence like *I only spoke to John* could imply either 'I didn't do anything else' or 'I didn't speak to anyone else'. In speech, however, there is no ambiguity: *only* goes with the most prominent word:

I only SPOKE to John. (I didn't give him anything)
I only spoke to JOHN. (and no one else)

People come to use prosody (p.236) naturally, as they learn to speak. Punctuation and other graphic conventions, however, have to be formally taught while learning to read and write.

Punctuation has two main functions:

- **It separates units of grammar**: for example, words are separated by a space, sentences by a combination of mark + space, paragraphs by a new start to a line.

- **It indicates a specific grammatical or other function**: for example, the apostrophe indicates the genitive ending (p.132) or the omission of a letter.

Usage

There are many differences in punctuation practice. American and British publishing traditions differ, as do individual publishers. Individual writers also differ in their preference for 'light' or 'heavy' punctuation, especially in the amount of use they make of the comma.

In fact I'll go in the old red bus this time. (light)
In fact, I'll go in the old, red bus, this time. (heavy)

This chapter corresponds to Chapter 76 in *Making Sense of Grammar* (see p.253).

The main punctuation conventions

- A sequence of **unseparated letters** identifies a word.

- The **hyphen** (-) joins parts of a word.

- The **space** separates words.

Hawker

- The **comma** (,) separates words, phrases, and some clauses.

- The **colon** (:) makes a more definite separation between a clause and what follows.

- The **semi-colon** (;) shows coordination, especially between clauses.

- The **full-stop** (.), **question-mark** (?) and **exclamation-mark** (!), along with an initial capital, separate sentences.

- A combination of sentence marks and space (especially the **indentation** of the first line) separates paragraphs.

- Several **pairs** of punctuation marks are available to show that one construction has been included within another: commas, dashes, parentheses, quotation marks.

The prize, a bottle of beer, was much appreciated.
The prize – a bottle of beer – was much appreciated.
The prize (a bottle of beer) was much appreciated.
I saw the words 'a bottle of beer' on the card.

Usage guide

'I miss the good old days when we all had to worry about was nouns and verbs.'

General index

Further reading

The main work to which this book relates is *A Comprehensive Grammar of the English Language* by R Quirk, S Greenbaum, G Leech and J Svartvik (Longman, 1985, 1779 pages). However, there are several smaller grammars, using the same basic approach, which can be consulted before tackling the detailed exposition found in the *Comprehensive*. *A Student's Grammar of the English Language* is an abridged version by Greenbaum and Quirk, published in 1990 (Longman, 490 pages). *A Grammar of Contemporary English* was published by the same authors in 1972 (Longman, 1120 pages). An abridged version of this, *A University Grammar of English,* was published by Quirk and Greenbaum in 1973 (Longman, 484 pages); and a version with the needs of foreign learners of English in mind, *A Communicative Grammar of English*, was published by Leech and Svartvik in a second edition in 1994 (Longman, 423 pages). There is also a workbook based on the *University Grammar* by R Close (*A University Grammar of English*: *Workbook*, Longman, 1975). But in consulting these earlier works, be prepared for minor changes in approach and terminology. On several questions of contemporary English usage see also my *Who Cares About English Usage?* (Penguin, 2000), and *The English Language* (Penguin, 1988, 2nd edn. 2002).

The next step

The above reading takes you deeper into the detail of English grammar. It does not, however, provide the kind of semantic and pragmatic perspective which, as my Preface suggested, is now offering an illuminating frame of reference for English language studies. This perspective, in my view, provides the bridge between the terminology and analysis which *Rediscover Grammar* introduces and the active use of grammar in language production and comprehension. It is systematically introduced in my *Making Sense of Grammar* (Longman, 2004), in which the approach of the present book is interpreted from semantic and pragmatic points of view, using the same topic breakdown, terminology, and chapter numbering.

Pearson Education
Edinburgh Gate
Harlow
Essex
CM20 2JE
England

ISBN-10: 0-582-84862-8
ISBN-13: 978-0-582-84862-7

First published 1988
Secon edition 1996
Third edition 2004
Fourth impression 2006
Set in Bell Gothic
Printed in China
SWTC/04

Acknowledgements

We are grateful to the following for permission to reproduce cartoons and other copyright material:
Express Newspaper / *Daily Star*, page 109 left; Maersk Air, page 38 lower; News Group Newspaper / *The Sun*, page 109 right; Punch Publications, pages 50, 67, 101, 185, 194, 245 and 247; Quirk et al. *A Comprehensive Grammar of the English Language*, Longman, 1985, page 192.
The publisher's policy is to use paper manufactured from sustainable forests.